The Art of
HELPING

Robert R. Carkhuff

FIFTH EDITION

Human Resource Development Press
Publishers of Human Technology

Copyright • 1983 by
Human Resource Development Press, Inc.
22 Amherst Road, Amherst, Massachusetts 01002
413-253-3488

Bernice R. Carkhuff, Publisher

Fifth Edition
Second Printing, August, 1984
Third Printing, February 1985

Library of Congress Cataloging in Publication Data

International Standard Book No. 0-914234-16-1

Illustrations by Krawczyk
Design by Dorothy Fall
Composition by The Magazine Group
Printing and Binding by Bookcrafters, Inc.

TABLE OF CONTENTS

PREFACE

In 1960, as a clinical intern, I saw my first client. I had completed my counseling and therapeutic courses. I knew a lot about the theory and practice of helping. But I did not know what to do.

I asked more experienced practitioners. Their answers varied, depending upon their orientations. One thing they all agreed upon, though, was that the helper had to attempt to understand the client. Yet, not one of them could tell me how to do it.

They offered little help in communicating understanding to a client. One orientation provided me with techniques that helped me to involve the client. Another provided techniques to identify the client's deeper meanings. Still another provided techniques for judging and deciding. And one provided techniques for developing and initiating courses of action.

Later, we studied these techniques to determine if there were any common ingredients (Appendix B). We researched and factored the helping process into responsive and initiative activities. We validated the applicability of these activities to helping people with problems of living, learning and working. We developed research to identify and then use the relationship of people's physical, emotional and intellectual functioning with their problems. But, above all, we studied how people really learn. In experiment after experiment we researched how people become involved in the helping process, explore their experience, understand their goals and take action to achieve their goals.

Those same experiments allowed us to find what skills the helper needs in order to facilitate the client through the helping process. This book describes and teaches those skills.

As we studied the helping process we discovered that helping was not bound by the four walls of a therapist's

office, nor by the minutes of a client-hour. Helping occurred whenever there was a responsive and initiative
interaction between people. Such interactions always
result in a person's growth. We stopped thinking in terms
of therapist and client. Instead, we started thinking in
terms of helper and helpee, members of the same team
whose relationship was oriented entirely to a human
being's growth. These are the terms used in this book.

Research Summary

Over a period of two decades we have refined the application of these helping dimensions in a variety of settings and with different populations. We have now summarized over 20 years of research involving people who
were recipients of these helping skills. The results were
illuminating. With over 160 studies of over 150,000 people, they indicate the efficacy of interpersonal helping
skills (See Appendix B).

The studies of the effects of helpers with high levels of
interpersonal skills upon indices of living, learning and
working effectiveness are 96% positive. The studies of
the direct effects of training helpees in interpersonal skills
upon indices of living, learning and working effectiveness
are also 96% positive.

This means that our chances of achieving any reasonable living, learning or working outcome are about 95%
when either helpers or helpees are trained in interpersonal helping skills. In other words, the chances of
achieving negative results for any projects involving high
levels of interpersonal skills training for either helpers or
helpees are random. Conversely, the chances of achieving any human goal without trained helpers or helpees
are random.

I initially distilled these skills programs twelve years ago
in the first edition of The Art of Helping. Now, five edi-
tions, and more than 200,000 readers later, we are
presenting Helping V. Our models of helping continue to

evolve. Yet the interpersonal core of helping remains the same. Just as our helping practices grow and change, so do we as helpers, teachers and trainers grow and change. As we continue to grow and change in our skills, so will our helpees, students and trainees grow and gain in their daily living, learning and working activities.

I am in particular debt to John R. Cannon, James T. Chapados and Richard M. Pierce for their contributions to *Helping V.* In addition, I am appreciative of the continuous support and administrative assistance of Bernice Carkhuff and Kathleen Bopp.

April, 1983   R.R.C.
Washington, D.C.

ABOUT THE AUTHOR

Dr. Robert R. Carkhuff is the most-referenced counseling psychologist according to Division 17, American Psychological Association. He is Chairman, Carkhuff Institute of Human Technology, a non-profit institute dedicated to the development and implementation of human resource development, training and performance programs in home, school, work and community settings.

The American Institute for Scientific Information ranks Dr. Carkhuff as the second youngest of the 100 most-cited social scientists, including such historical figures as Dewey, Freud and Marx. He is also author of three of the 100 most-referenced texts, including his two-volume classic, *Helping and Human Relations*.

Dr. Carkhuff is known as the originator of helping models and human resource development skills programs. He is also parent of the Human Technology™ movement which emphasizes models, systems and technologies for individual performance and organizational productivity. His most recent book on the topics of human resource development and productivity is *Sources of Human Productivity*.

1
Introduction and Overview

We are born with the potential to grow - no more - no less! Those of us who learn to actualize this potential will know lives of untold fullness and excitement. We will develop growth responses that will enable us to go anywhere and do anything. Those of us who do not learn to actualize this potential will know lives of waste and tragedy.

From the moment we enter the world to the instant we exit this life, we experience opportunities for growth. Regardless of our condition, anytime between our birth and our death, each of us has the potential for growth.

Growth can be physical, emotional and intellectual. Physical growth is an improvement in our blood, bone and tissue. More specifically, we may measure increases in our strength, flexibility, coordination and endurance.

Emotional growth is an improvement in our ability to relate to ourselves and our worlds. We may measure our emotional functioning by our levels of motivation in relation to our performances in various areas of our lives. We may also measure our emotional functioning by the number and quality of interpersonal relationships we maintain.

Intellectual growth is an improvement in our knowledge and skills. Such growth may be measured by our mastery of our substance and our ability to learn and teach.

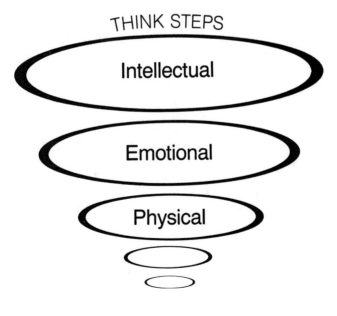

THINK STEPS

Intellectual

Emotional

Physical

GROWING

When we grow, we improve our functioning in various areas of our lives. We begin to live more effectively in our homes with our families and in our communities with our friends and neighbors. We also begin to learn more effectively in our schools and training centers with our classmates, teachers and learners. Finally, we begin to work more effectively in our workplaces with our co-workers, bosses and employees. When we grow physically, emotionally and intellectually, we function effectively in the living, learning and working areas of our lives.

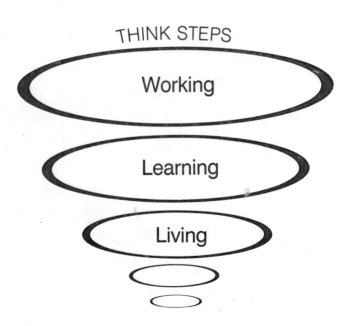

THINK STEPS

Working

Learning

Living

FUNCTIONING

The most fundamental human characteristic is the ability to learn. It is the human characteristic that makes it possible for us to grow and function effectively in our lives. It is the human characteristic that distinguishes us from all other forms of life.

Learning is the ability to transform a stimulus or input into a response or output. For example, we may respond to the baby's cry or write about our experience. In responding to the baby's cry, we are usually making a conditioned or habitual response. This means that we are associating our response to the stimulus without thinking. When we write about our experience, we may process the stimulus to communicate a response. This means that we are thinking about the response we are going to make to the stimulus experience.

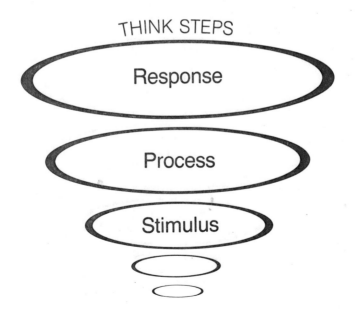

THINK STEPS

Response

Process

Stimulus

LEARNING

When we think about the response we are going to make, we say that we are processing. Initially, processing involves exploring where we are in relation to the experience. Transitionally, processing involves understanding where we want or need to be. Finally, processing involves acting to get to where we want to be. For example, in writing this material, I explored my experience in relation to the effective ingredients of helping. Transitionally, I understood my goals for writing as communicating helping skills to you, the reader. Finally, I acted to write my outlines, texts and revisions needed to communicate the helping skills.

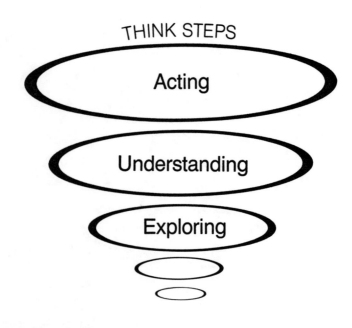

THINK STEPS

Acting

Understanding

Exploring

PROCESSING

Human Processing

The helping process is another instance of human processing or learning. It is useful to think of helping as either a learning or relearning process. We are helpful when we engage someone in a learning process that guides them and prevents problems as, for example, guidance counselors do. We are also helpful when we engage someone in a relearning process that rehabilitates them or solves problems as, for example, rehabilitation specialists do. In both guidance or rehabilitation the helping process involves the phases of processing: exploring; understanding; acting.

Before helpees can engage in processing, they must become involved. Involving is a pre-helping phase. Helpees become involved by preparing themselves physically, emotionally and intellectually. Physically, they become involved in helping by assuming an attentive posture to the experience and the helper. Emotionally, they become involved by being motivated to change in their functioning or gain in their growth. They also become emotionally involved by relating interpersonally to the experience and the helper. Intellectually, they become involved by learning all of the skills they need to be helped effectively, i.e., the skills of exploring, understanding and acting that you will study now.

PRE-PROCESSING

Involving

INVOLVING IN THE PROCESS

Exploring is the first phase of the helping process. Exploring involves two phases: analyzing our experience and diagnosing ourselves in relation to our experience. Analyzing our experience emphasizes breaking it down into its critical parts. Diagnosing ourselves emphasizes assessing our functioning in relation to the critical parts of our experience.

For example, if we have interpersonal problems with loved ones, we may find that we did not know how to relate to them. Our inability to relate might have led readily to our interpersonal problems. Exploring our experience prepares us for understanding our experience.

PHASES OF PROCESSING

PRE   I

Involving ➡️ Exploring

EXPLORING EXPERIENCE

Understanding is the second phase of the helping process. Understanding also involves two phases: developing and personalizing our goals. Developing our goals is based upon our diagnosis: our goal is usually the next level above our diagnosed level of functioning. Personalizing our goals emphasizes internalizing the goals or making them ours.

For example, if we have learning problems with one of our subjects in school, we may find that we do not know the principles involved in applying our knowledge or skills. We may then develop and personalize our goal of learning how to develop the principles. Understanding the goal prepares us for acting to achieve the goal.

PHASES OF PROCESSING

PRE   I   II

Involving ➤ Exploring ➤ Understanding

UNDERSTANDING GOALS

Acting is the third phase of the helping process. Acting also emphasizes two phases: defining our goals and developing our programs. Defining our goals emphasizes the operations involved in the goals. Developing our programs emphasizes the steps needed to achieve the goals.

For example, if we have performance problems at our work stations, we may find that we do not have clear expectancies of how well we are to perform our tasks. We may develop our programs to elicit input from our supervisors concerning their measurable expectancies for our performance. Acting upon the program prepares us for recycling the phases of processing.

PHASES OF PROCESSING

PRE   I   II   III

Involving➡Exploring➡Understanding➡Acting

ACTING UPON PROGRAMS

The phases of processing are recycled. When we implement the steps of our programs, we receive feedback from our environment in acting. For example, our friends or loved ones may provide us feedback in our interpersonal relations. Our test results may provide us feedback in our learning area. Our supervisors may provide us with a performance appraisal at work. This feedback recycles the processing. It stimulates more extensive exploration of our experience, more accurate understanding of our goals and more effective acting upon our programs. This processing continues as we improve in functioning. This processing continues in an upward, spiraling cycle of life for the growing person.

PHASES OF PROCESSING

PRE   I   II   III

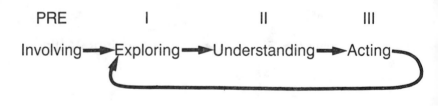

Involving⟶Exploring⟶Understanding⟶Acting

RECYCLING THE PROCESS

The helping process emphasizes the skills effective helpers employ to facilitate the learning or relearning process. We think of the recipients of helping as helpees. We may say that the only difference between the helpers and the helpees is who they "r". Who you are is a function of the skills you have. Effective helpers have skills to facilitate their helpees' movement through the phases of processing.

Effective helpers are fully attentive so as to involve their helpees in processing. They respond accurately to facilitate their helpees' exploring of their experiences. They personalize their helpees' understanding of their goals. They initiate and individualize their helpees' action programs. Effective helpers are both models and agents for their helpees' growth. They provide the helping experiences that enable the helpees to become helpers.

THE HELPING PROCESS

2
Attending —
Involving the Helpee

Newborn infants enter the world with little other than reflex responses: the sucking reflex and the palmar or grasping reflex, for example. If people in the environment attend to the children, these reflexes will become instrumental to their survival. The children will be able to nurse with their sucking reflexes. The children will be able to grasp things with their palmar reflexes.

In the beginning, however, newborn infants bring little but their inherent resources to their worlds. In their utter dependency, they wait upon us to insure their survival by attending to their needs. Gradually, we guide them to the things they need to have to maintain themselves. Gradually, staying attuned to their needs, we involve them directly with their worlds. In so doing, we involve them in learning about themselves and their worlds.

Here are some questions that you can ask as you begin to think about attending:

How do you know when someone is really interested in you?

How do you know when someone is being attentive toward you?

What can you learn about people by looking at them?

How do you know when someone is really listening to you?

Case Study #1—Nonattending

Katherine is a 20-year-old college student. She has called Joyce, an acquaintance, "to get together and talk". Katherine wants Joyce's advice. Joyce is twenty-one years old and just finishing a Bachelor of Arts in psychology.

Joyce was not sure why Katherine called her. They were certainly not friends. Joyce doubted if Katherine ever had a close friend. Katherine exasperated people. Joyce and her friends had talked about it several times. No one was sure why Katherine affected people this way. She seemed nice enough, but something about her irritated people.

Joyce was regretting her appointment with Katherine. She really hadn't wanted to see her. On top of that, everything that could go wrong had gone wrong that day. The weather was hot and humid. The bus broke down on the way home so she had to walk the last two miles. Her air conditioner was broken and she didn't have time for a bath before Katherine would arrive. All she could think of was how tired and hungry she was and how badly she did not want to see Katherine. As Joyce was thinking this very thought, the doorbell rang.

Joyce: (distractedly) "Hi, Katherine, come on in." (Joyce walks into the bedroom signalling Katherine to follow. Once there, she starts to change. Katherine stands in the doorway, watching.) "I hope your day was better than mine." (Katherine says nothing. After changing clothes, Joyce leads the way into the living room. Katherine sits on the couch. Joyce takes a chair across the coffee table from her. Joyce lights a cigarette with a deep breath, then exhales.) "Now, what did you want to talk about?"

Katherine: "I. . .I'm not sure where to begin. Well, I just can't seem to make friends. Nobody seems to like me. I. . ."

Joyce: "Oh, come on! I'm your friend. Listen, Katherine, I think you're just too sensitive."

Katherine: "I don't know. No one seems to care."

Joyce: "Would I be talking to you if I didn't care?"

Katherine: (hesitantly) "Nooo. . .but. . ."

Joyce: (interrupting) "Maybe the problem is you're too uptight, you know what I mean? You never seem to be able to loosen up."

Katherine: "I don't know, Joyce. I just feel. . .lonely. I hardly ever have a date and when I do they never ask me out again."

Joyce: "Well, maybe if you fixed yourself up a little bit. You know. . .look more available."

Katherine: "I don't know what you mean."

Joyce: "Come on now, Katherine. If you want to get to know someone you have to let him know you're interested. I'm not talking about being cheap."

Katherine: "I don't know."

Joyce: "Come on, Katherine. You said you were lonely. I've got an idea. Let's go dancing tomorrow night. I have a lot going on tonight, but let's go tomorrow. I'll call you tomorrow to set the time and stuff, okay?" (Joyce stands up and heads for the door. Katherine looks at her.) "I wish I could talk some more, Katherine, but I've got to get crackin'."

Katherine: (as she stands up, looking confused) "Oh, sure."

Joyce: (leaning against the door after Katherine has left, muttering in a low voice) "Why do I get talked into these things?"

Attending is the necessary pre-condition of helping. To understand its critical nature, you may turn away from others in your presence. Ask yourself how you communicate interest in the others. More important, how do you learn about or from the others? As you turn gradually toward the others, you will learn about them. You will learn primarily by what you see and what you hear.

Attending skills posture the helper to see and hear the helpees. They involve preparing for helping, attending personally, observing and listening. Attending skills serve to involve the helpees in helping. When the helper is fully attentive, the helpees become fully attentive and engage in the helping process. Attending lays the base for responding to facilitate helpee exploration.

ATTENDING INVOLVES THE HELPEE

While the emphasis during the pre-helping phase is upon attending, this dimension takes place in the context of a core of conditions that will change over the course of helping. Primary among these core conditions is the dimension of empathy. Empathy emphasizes entering the frames of reference of others. We will learn more about empathy when we address responding. For now, it is most productive to conceive of attending to the needs of the helpees as the most basic level of empathy.

Respect is another core condition. Respect emphasizes communicating regard for the ability of others to manage their own lives. Initially, respect is incorporated within empathy as when we suspend our own frames of reference in concentrating upon the helpees. During this phase, we communicate our formal regard for the helpees' potential. As helping continues, respect becomes increasingly differentiated as the helper tries to reinforce the helpees' process movement toward growing.

Genuineness is a critical core condition. At its highest levels, genuineness involves being fully and freely ourselves. It is what the helpees search to become—genuine. However, initially we emphasize a pleasant and polite helper. We are very cautious about making the helpees feel insecure by anything that we might do or share. We will become increasingly genuine over the course of helping.

Finally, concreteness is an important core condition. Concreteness is simply the specificity with which we treat the helpees' experiences. Initially, we are specific only in regard to attending to the helpees' needs. Gradually, we will become more specific as the helpees explore their experiences.

THE CORE CONDITIONS OF INVOLVING

PRE-HELPING PHASE

HELPER DIMENSIONS	SKILLS LEVEL EMPHASIS
Empathy	Attending to Needs
Respect	Suspending Frame of Reference
Genuineness	Communicating Self Cautiously
Concreteness	Meeting Concrete Needs
	↓
HELPEE PROCESS	INVOLVING

PRE-HELPING CORE SKILLS

Preparing for Attending

The first task in attending is preparing for attending. Like preparation for anything in life, preparing is a necessary but not sufficient condition of involving the helpees. Preparing for attending involves preparing the helpees, the context and the helpers. If the helpees are not prepared to make the contact, they will not appear. If the context is not prepared to receive the helpees, they will not return. If the helpers are not prepared to attend to the helpees, they will not become involved in the helping process. Preparing for attending prepares us for attending personally to the helpees.

The helpees' willingness to become involved will depend upon how well we prepare them for the helping interaction. Preparing the helpees involves engaging them, informing them of our availability and encouraging them to use our help.

Engaging the helpees emphasizes greeting them formally and establishing a common frame of reference concerning the purpose of the contact.

Informing the helpees emphasizes communicating the following data:

Who they will be seeing.

When and where the appointments will take place.

How to get there.

What the general purpose of the contact will be.

Encouraging the helpees emphasizes providing the helpees with the reasons for becoming involved by answering the following questions:

Why should I get involved?

Why do you want to get involved with me?

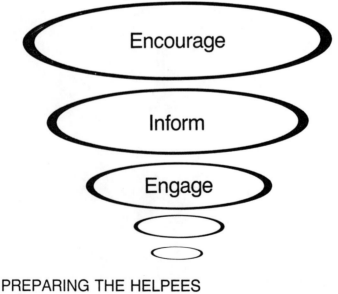

THINK STEPS

Encourage

Inform

Engage

PREPARING THE HELPEES

Our ability to facilitate helpee involvement also depends in part upon preparing the context for the helpee. Preparing the context involves arranging the furniture and decorations and organizing our offices or meeting rooms.

Arranging the furniture emphasizes facilitating open communication by sitting in chairs, facing each other with no desks, tables or other barriers between them. If there are several helpees, the chairs should be placed in a circle to facilitate the communication of interest and attentiveness to one another.

Arranging decorations emphasizes utilizing decorations to which the helpees can relate. For instance, if the helpees are college students, our decorations should reflect things that are familiar and comfortable to them.

Finally, the helping setting needs to be organized in a neat and orderly fashion. That way we communicate that we are on top of our own affairs and ready to focus upon the problems of the helpees.

THINK STEPS

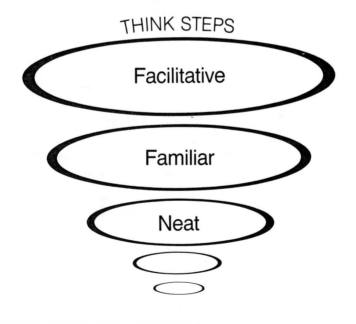

Facilitative

Familiar

Neat

PREPARING THE CONTEXT

It is as important to prepare ourselves for helping as it is to prepare our helpees and the context. We prepare ourselves by reviewing what we know about the helpees and the goal of helping as well as by relaxing ourselves.

Reviewing what we know about helping emphasizes reminding ourselves of what we know about the helpees from all previous interactions. This information may include formal notes, intake data and records as well as informal impressions.

Reviewing the helping goals emphasizes the purpose of the contacts. During the initial stages of helping, the goals will be to involve the helpees in exploring their experiences of their problems.

Relaxing ourselves emphasizes relaxing our minds and bodies prior to the actual helping interactions. Some helpers relax their minds by thinking of pleasant, soothing experiences. Others relax their bodies by physically relaxing one set of muscles after the other. We must experiment and find the method of relaxing that is most effective for us.

THINK STEPS

Reviewing Information

Reviewing Goals

Relaxing

PREPARING OURSELVES

Attending Personally

Preparing for attending enables us to attend personally to the helpees. By attending personally we bring our helpees into close proximity with us. In so doing, we communicate our interest in the helpees. Communicating an interest in the helpees tends to elicit a reciprocal response of interest from the helpees.

Attending personally involves posturing ourselves to give our full and undivided attention to the helpees. Attending personally emphasizes facing the helpees fully by squaring with them, leaning forward or toward them and making eye contact with them. Attending personally to the helpees prepares us for observing them fully.

One way of posturing ourselves to attend to the helpees is to face them fully. Whether standing or sitting, we may attend to an individual helpee by facing him or her squarely—our left shoulder to the helpee's right shoulder and vice versa. When we are dealing with a couple or a small group of people, we should place ourselves at the point of a right angle drawn from the people to our extreme left and right. See how differently we feel about the helpees when we posture ourselves in this manner from how we feel when we posture ourselves for purposes of our own comfort.

SQUARING

There are other ways of posturing ourselves to attend personally. The inclination of our bodies is one critical way. For example, when we are sitting we attend most fully when we incline our bodies forward or toward the helpees to a point where we can rest our forearms on our thighs. When standing, we attend most fully when we close the physical distance by moving closer to the helpees. Putting one leg in front of the other will help us to lean slightly toward the helpees.

There are still other ways of attending to **people** in need of help.

LEANING

We must seek in every way possible to communicate our full and undivided attention. Perhaps the key way of attending personally involves how we use our senses, particularly our eyes. We communicate attentiveness when we maintain eye contact with the helpees. The helpees are aware of our efforts to make contact with them psychologically through our efforts to make contact with them visually.

MAKING EYE CONTACT

One way of structuring personal attending while sitting is to view ourselves in terms of the skills involved. Indeed, we may rate ourselves as follows according to our demonstration of the skills.

High attending — Squared, eye contact, and leaning 20 degrees or more

Moderate attending — Squared, eye contact

Low attending — Not squared, slouching

LEVELS OF PERSONAL ATTENDING WHILE SITTING

Clearly, we do not always attend personally by sitting.
Often we are attempting to help people while standing.
We can use a similar scale to rate our demonstration of
the skills while standing.

High attending — Squared, eye contact, and leaning 10 degrees

Moderate attending — Squared, eye contact

Low attending — Not squared

LEVELS OF PERSONAL ATTENDING WHILE STANDING

We communicate personal attending by all of our man-
nerisms and expressions. When we are intense but relaxed, we communicate attentiveness. When we are ner-
vous and fidgety, we communicate reluctance to be
there. When we are consistent in attentive behavior, we
communicate interest. When we blush or turn pale, we
communicate different levels of reaction to the helpees. It
is important to have ourselves "together" in attending
behavior.

We can practice our own attending posture, first in front
of a mirror and then with people we see in everyday life
to whom we want to communicate interest and concern.
We may feel awkward at first; after awhile, however, we
should notice that we focus more upon the other person
and that the other person is more attentive to us.

COMMUNICATING INTEREST

Observing

Perhaps the most important skill that personal attending prepares us for is observing. Observing skills are the most basic helping skills. They are the source of our greatest learning about the helpees. When all else fails, we emphasize observing our helpees. We learn most of what we need to know about people by observing them.

We learn about our helpees' energy levels by observing them physically. We learn about our helpees' feelings by observing them emotionally. We learn about our helpees' readiness for involvement by observing them intellectually. Observing our helpees prepares us for listening to them.

The most important thing that we can know about our helpees is their level of energy. Energy level is the amount of physical effort put into purposeful tasks. Knowing how long people can sustain high levels of functioning is essential to knowing how people experience their lives. Only people with high energy levels can experience the fullness of life. Persons with low energy levels have great difficulty in meeting even the simplest demands of everyday life.

We can observe energy level in three principal areas: body build, posture and grooming. For example, helpees who are physically overweight or underweight or whose muscle tone is poor will tend to have low levels of energy. In addition, helpees with slouched postures are assuming postures that suggest low energy. Finally, helpees who fail to present clean and neat appearances usually do not have the energy to maintain themselves.

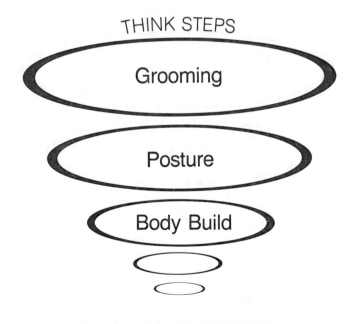

THINK STEPS

Grooming

Posture

Body Build

OBSERVING PHYSICAL DIMENSIONS

The emotional level will show us the helpees' feelings. A high emotional level means the helpees have enough "up" feelings to relate effectively to the tasks at hand. A low emotional level means "down" feelings and poor task performance.

We can observe emotional level in three specific areas: postural, behavioral and facial expressions. Postural dimensions emphasize indications of depression or tension. For example, drooped shoulders and head may indicate "down" feelings while rigidity of posture and tight musculature are indicators of tension. Behavioral dimensions reflect similar indicators, with slow movements indicating "down" feelings and overly-swift gestures suggesting tension. We can make similar inferences from the basic facial expressions of happiness, surprise, fear, anger, sadness, contempt and interest.

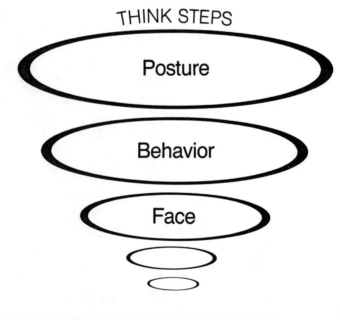

THINK STEPS

Posture

Behavior

Face

OBSERVING EMOTIONAL DIMENSIONS

Ultimately, the dimension that distinguishes humans from all other forms of life is our intellect. A high level of intellectual readiness means that the helpees are prepared to focus upon their tasks while a low level means that they are not.

We can observe intellectual level in the same three specific areas: postural, behavioral and facial expressions. For example, slouched postures positioned "away" from the learning experience may indicate a lack of readiness for processing. Similarly, nonpurposeful behavioral expressions may indicate movement "away" from learning. Finally, facial expressions will indicate the level of focus of interest upon the experience at hand.

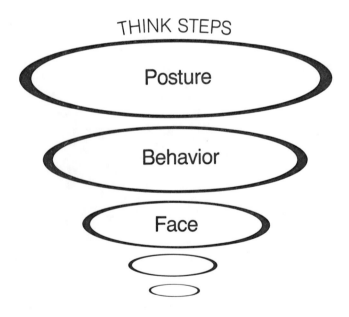

THINK STEPS

Posture

Behavior

Face

OBSERVING INTELLECTUAL DIMENSIONS

One way of structuring observing is to observe the helpees for precisely the same attending posture which we tried to exhibit as helpers. These observational inferences will help guide us in interpreting the behavior we are observing. We can complement these inferences with the richness of other observations. We can make inferences about the helpees' functioning from these data as follows:

LEVELS OF ATTENDING

AREA	LOW ATTENDING	MODERATE ATTENDING	HIGH ATTENDING
Physical	Low Energy	Moderate Energy	High Energy
Emotional	Down Feeling	Mixed Feelings	Up Feelings
Intellectual	Low Readiness	Moderate Readiness	High Readiness

LEVELS OF INFERRING FROM OBSERVATIONS

Perhaps one of the most important observations we can make is of discrepancies or incongruencies in people's behavior or appearance. Being incongruent simply means that people are not consistent in different aspects of their behavior or appearance. For example, people may say they feel fine while sitting slumped, looking at the floor and fidgeting.

Being incongruent is itself a critical sign of people in trouble. Helpees invariably want to become more positively congruent. Perhaps the most important aspect of behavior to which you can respond initially is the helpees' desire to get themselves "together". More than anything else in the world, the helpees want to be able to function effectively without those glaring inconsistencies in their actions.

OBSERVING INCONGRUENCIES

We can observe ourselves in the same manner that we observe others. What does our appearance and behavior say about us? Do we project a high level of energy, feeling and readiness to help? Are we congruent in our behavior and our expressed desire to help?

We can also use our observations of ourselves and our helpees to involve the helpees in helping. In helping, we should be focusing our entire beings upon the helpees and their expressions of their experience. In this manner, we are communicating nonverbally that we are attending to them and focused in our interest in their experiences of themselves. In so doing, we increase the helpees' sense of comfort and security in helping.

OBSERVING OURSELVES

Listening

The sources of input that we most often employ in helping are the verbal expressions of the helpees. What people say and how they say it tells us a lot about how they
see themselves and the world around them. Ultimately,
the helpees' verbal expressions are the richest source of
empathic understanding for the helper.

When we give the helpees our full and undivided attention, we are prepared for listening to their verbal expressions. The more we attend to the external cues presented
by the helpees, the more we can listen to the internal
cues reflecting their inner experiences. There are many
ways that we can develop our listening skills. These include having a reason for listening, suspending our judgment, focusing upon the helpee and the content, and
recalling the expression while listening for common
themes. Listening prepares us for responding empathic-
ally to our helpees.

OBSERVING➡LISTENING

First, as listeners, we should know why we are listening. We should have a reason for listening. The goal of helping is the reason for listening: gathering all of the information that we can related to the problems or goals presented by the helpees.

As with observing, we should listen for cues to the helpees' levels of physical, emotional and intellectual functioning. To do this, we must focus not only upon the words but also upon the tone of voice and the manner of presentation. The words will tell us the intellectual content of the helpees' experiences. The tone of voice will tell us about the helpees' attendant feelings. The manner of presentation will tell us about the helpees' energy levels. For example, content expressed in a dull tone of voice and in a listless manner suggests a depressed helpee with a low level of energy.

THINK STEPS

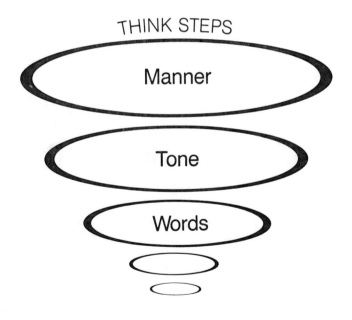

HAVING A REASON FOR LISTENING

Next, it is important to suspend our own personal judgments in listening, at least initially. If we are going to listen to what the helpees say, we must temporarily suspend the things which we say to ourselves. We must let the helpees' messages sink in without trying to make decisions about them.

Suspending judgment means suspending our values and attitudes regarding the content of the helpees' expressions. For example, we may not approve of the helpees' behaviors or the way they are living their lives. However, our feelings are not relevant to the helpees' experiences and our purpose is to facilitate the helpees' growth and development. In addition, we must exercise caution in offering premature solutions, no matter how many times we think we have been over this ground with others. Each helpee has a unique experience, and it is our job to allow the uniqueness of that experience to emerge.

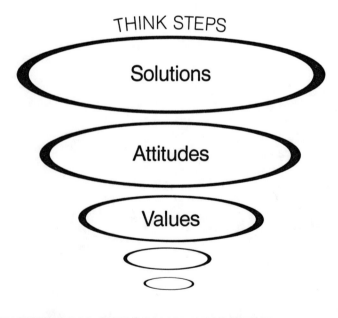

THINK STEPS

Solutions

Attitudes

Values

SUSPENDING PERSONAL JUDGMENT

Perhaps the most important thing in listening is to focus upon the helpees. We focus upon the helpees by resisting distractions. Just as we initially resist the judgmental voice within ourselves, so must we also resist outside distractions. There will always be a lot of things going on that will not help us to listen.

We must place ourselves in quiet places so that we can focus upon the helpees' inner experiences. To the degree that we can, we must use a helping context that avoids noises, views and people—anything or anyone that will take our attention away from the helpees to whom we are listening. We must summon all of our energy, affect and intellect to focus upon the helpees' inner experiences and external behaviors so that we can respond accurately to those experiences and behaviors.

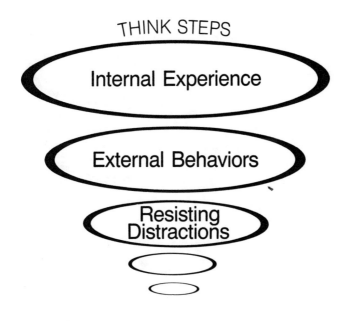

THINK STEPS

Internal Experience

External Behaviors

Resisting Distractions

FOCUSING UPON THE HELPEES

In listening to the helpees, we focus initially upon the content. In focusing upon the content, we want to be sure that we have all of the details of the helpees' experiences. Otherwise we will not be able to help them to understand their experiences. We focus upon content by making sure that we have covered all of the 5WH basic interrogatives:

Who?
What?
Why?
When?
Where?
How?

By answering these questions, we can be sure that we have the basic ingredients of the content of the helpees' experiences.

FOCUSING UPON THE CONTENT

We should concentrate intensely enough upon the helpees' expressions to be able to recall both the content and the affect of the expression. With brief expressions we should recall the entire expression verbatim. With lengthy expressions, we should try to recall the gist of the expression. You might try now to recall the following expression of a young man in trouble:

"Things are not going so good for me. Not in school. Not with my girl. I just seem to be floundering. I fake it every day but inside I'm really down because I'm not sure of what I want to do or where I want to go."

Now practice your listening skills in recalling the expression. What are the cues to the young man's energy level and feeling state? What are the 5WHs of his experience? What are the "gaps" in his expression? All of these cues will be the bases for later exploration in helping.

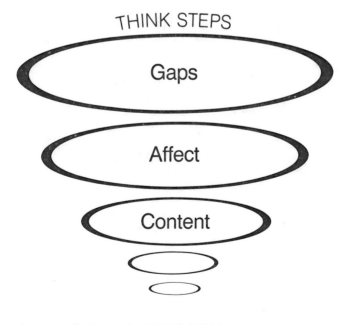

THINK STEPS

Gaps

Affect

Content

RECALLING THE EXPRESSION

We must also learn to recall the helpees' expressions over a period of time. In so doing, we are looking for the common themes in the helpees' experiences. The helpees' important themes will be repeated over and over. Usually, the helpees will invest the most intensity in these themes because they are trying to communicate them to us.

These themes will tell us what the helpees are really trying to say about themselves and their worlds. They will tell us where they are "coming from" if we just provide them the opportunity. We need only receive the messages they are sending and process them for the common themes to prepare ourselves for responding to the helpees.

We should practice listening for themes in our daily conversations. For now, we can use the case studies at the beginning and end of each chapter. See how well we do when compared to the helpers involved.

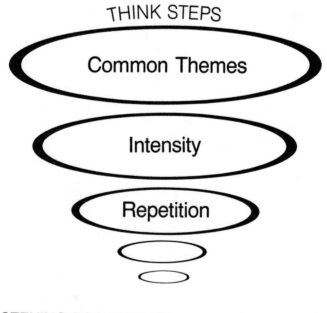

THINK STEPS

Common Themes

Intensity

Repetition

LISTENING FOR THEMES

There is no question that listening is hard work. It requires intense concentration. However, just as there are different rates for reading, so are there also different rates for listening. Most people talk at the rate of 100 to 150 words a minute. Yet we can easily listen at a rate of two or three times that amount. We can put this extra time to use by reflecting upon or thinking about what the helpees have said.

Most of us have been taught not to listen or to hear. Years of conditioning have gone into this. We are distracted because we do not want to hear. We distort the expressions because of the implications of understanding. Most of all, there are the implications for intimacy that make people fearful. Just as we have been conditioned not to listen or hear, now we must train ourselves to actively listen and hear.

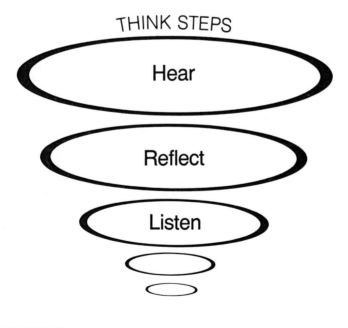

THINK STEPS

Hear

Reflect

Listen

HEARING

One of the ways of structuring listening is to test our verbatim recall of the people's expressions. Simply listen to these expressions and try to repeat verbatim what you heard. We may practice in live interactions or with written or taped expressions. We may rate the accuracy of our recall as follows:

High accuracy — Verbatim recall of expression

Moderate accuracy — Recall of gist of expression

Low accuracy — Little or no recall of expression

In the end, the entire verbal helping process hangs on our ability to listen and process the content and affect of the helpees' expressions.

LEVELS OF LISTENING

Now we can begin to build our own cumulative rating scale for helping. If the helper is attending personally, observing and listening to the helpees, we may rate the helper as fully attentive (level 2.0). If the helper is only attending personally, then the helper is rated at a less than fully attentive level (level 1.5). If the helper is not attending personally, then the helper cannot be rated in relation to the helpee (level 1.0).

LEVELS OF HELPING

5.0	
4.5	
4.0	
3.5	
3.0	
2.5	
2.0	Observing and listening
1.5	Attending personally
1.0	Nonattending

LEVELS OF HELPING—ATTENDING

If we have attended to the helpees effectively, then we will have involved them in helping. The helpees will experience comfort in the preparations we made for them. They will experience security in our attentiveness and confidence in our observations. They will begin to share their experiences and we will have the opportunity to listen and hear their expressions.

Above all else, the helpees will begin to reciprocate by involving themselves in the helping process. They will prepare for their sessions. They will become attentive and observant of themselves and others. They will begin to share their experiences and listen in turn to the expressions of others. In so doing, the helpees will signal us of their readiness to enter the exploratory phase of helping.

PHASES OF HELPING

PRE

HELPER: Attending

↓

HELPEE: INVOLVING

FACILITATING INVOLVING

Like any other set of skills, you will want to practice the attending skills until you have integrated them into your helping personality as has the helper in the following case study.

Case Study #2—Skilled Attending

Terry is a 23-year-old male who is tall, broad-shouldered and well-muscled. He appeared to be agitated and angry. When Paula, the therapist, first met Terry it was at her office. Her only preparation was a phone call from a company where she had a contract to provide employee assistance counseling asking her for an emergency appointment for Terry that afternoon.

When Paula walked into the waiting room she was surprised. Terry did not look like her typical client. He was tall, muscular and moved quickly. He wore work clothes, clean but obviously used for their purpose. And he was angry. He was pacing back and forth, his face contorted with the effort of controlling his rage. After hesitating a fraction of a second, she approached.

Paula: (reminding herself to stay relaxed) "Good morning. You must be Mr. Mason."

Terry: "Yeah."

Paula: (extending her hand) "My name is Paula Rantoul." (Terry takes her hand with a grasp which threatens to smash her fingers but turns out to be just a firm handshake.) "Please come into my office. Take the chair by the window; it's the most comfortable." (As Terry sits down Paula offers a cup of coffee which he refuses. Paula sits in a chair opposite Terry, leaning forward.) "Now, I understand you want to see me about some things that are troubling you."

Terry: "---damn right! I just lost my job because I hit

my foreman! If I don't learn how to control my temper my whole life will turn to sh--!'' (Paula leans forward a little more and looks at Terry frankly.) ''I don't know what a little girl like you can do to help me, but I'm ready to give anything a try!''

On he talked for another fifteen minutes, non-stop. Once he jumped up and started pacing, slamming his fist into his hand again and again as he talked. Paula stayed in her chair, turning to face him as he walked back and forth. When he realized what he was doing he smiled sheepishly and sat back down. Finally he stopped his tirade and sitting back in the chair looked at Paula sitting across from him.

Terry: ''You know, you got real guts. Most women would have high tailed it out of here or tried to get me to sit still. Why not you?''

Paula: (quietly, looking at Terry) ''You don't need another person to be afraid of you nor do you need a mother to criticize you right now. You said you want someone to help you. I've got to find out who you are first if I'm going to be that person. I can't do that if I'm running from you or trying to get you to do what I want.''

Terry: (looking baffled for a minute, then smiling) ''You really know what you're doing. You'll do.''

Paula: (smiling back) ''You're too powerful for me to treat self-indulgently. You're too powerful to treat yourself self-indulgently.''

Terry: ''You know you're right. I don't want to be out of control. All it does is get me into trouble.''

It took every one of Paula's attending skills to maintain contact with Terry. She had to attend contextually by preparing herself, the environment and Terry for the interaction. She did that by keeping her tension in control, putting Terry at ease, and by making her office as comfortable and yet as constructive as she could for her interaction with Terry. She made sure she kept good eye contact. She leaned forward and kept herself squared to Terry, even when he was pacing back and forth. She made observations that helped her to recognize that Terry was in control of his anger, but only barely. And she listened to what he was saying, trying to get information for future use.

Her efforts paid off. Her consistent use of attending skills resulted in having Terry commit himself to working with her, recognizing that she could help him grow.

3
Responding —
Facilitating Helpee
Exploring

Human learning and human intelligence begin to manifest themselves when children are several months old. At this point, the children begin to explore themselves and their environments. Children begin to discover the existence of environmental stimuli and their own responses and the relationships between these two. In other words, the children become aware of the association between the stimuli and their responses. They become aware of causes and effects in their worlds.

This awareness is a two-way street. For example, the children become aware that the nipple or the food serves as stimulus to sucking or grasping responses. The responses, in turn, will lead to satisfying needs for nourishment. The children may also become aware that need for nourishment stimulates the responses of searching for nipples or food.

By exploring, then, children become aware of both their past and present relationships to their environments—including themselves. The children are, in effect, attempting to recognize where they are in relation to their worlds. This is the first stage or phase of human learning. This awareness stage distinguishes humankind from all other forms of life.

Here are some questions that you can ask as you begin to think about responding:

How do you know when you can trust someone?

How do you know when somone has heard you?

How do you know if someone really understands you?

Case Study #3—Unskilled Responding

Matthew Benning is a 76-year-old man who had just been admitted to a nursing home. Up until now he had lived in his own home, a home he built himself fifty years ago. He lived there with his wife, raising four children. His children have all married and have left the area. His wife died two years ago.

Matt had to give up his home after a stroke partially paralyzed his left side. He can talk but needs a wheel-chair to get about.

He had been assigned to Carla's floor. Carla is the nursing supervisor for that floor. She has worked at the nursing home ever since she got her R.N. degree six years ago. She tries to be a good nurse and makes sure her staff is "as considerate as possible" of the patients. Following is an excerpt of a conversation between the two of them just after Matt arrived. The conversation took place in Matt's room which he shares with another patient.

Carla: (to Matt's roommate) "Hi Paul. I see you've got a new roommate."

Paul: "Yeah."

Carla: "I'm sure you are going to get along just fine." (to Matt) "Mr. Benning?"
(Matt is lying on the bed, eyes closed. He stirs and open his eyes.)

Carla: "Mr. Benning, my name is Carla Pope. I'm your nurse. How are you doing?"

Matt: "Huh?" (He sits up on the side of the bed with difficulty because of his left arm and leg.)

Carla: "How are you doing?"

Matt: "Oh fine, fine! Who did you say you were?"

Carla: "My name is Carla. I'm your nurse."

Matt: "Hi, my name is Matt Benning."

Carla: "Yes, I know. May I call you Matt?"

Matt: "Sure."

Carla: "Is there anything you would like?"

Matt: "Uh, no, I don't think so."
(Carla sits on the bed next to Matt.)

Carla: "You're sure?"

Matt: "No, I'm not, but I can't think of anything right now. Say, how long will I have to stay here?"

Carla: "Well that's hard to say. Besides you just got here." (cheerfully) "What's wrong? Don't you like us?"

Matt: "No, no! It's just that I've been away from home for so long. I've got so much to do. I've got to. . . ."

Carla: "Now don't worry about that. I'm sure that everything is just fine. What you need to think about is resting and getting better. Think of this as a vacation. Right, Paul?"

Paul: "Huh, what did you say?"

Carla: "Say, have you two met?"

Matt: "No, not yet."

Carla: "Well, since you're going to be roommates. I think you ought to." (cheerfully) "Paul Dobbs, meet Matt Benning."
(Both hesitantly smile and nod to each other.)

Matt: "Hi."

Paul: "Hello."

Carla: "Now, I'm just going to check on dinner and let you two get acquainted. Matt, I'll stop in later to see how you're doing. Paul, you might want to give Matt a cook's tour after dinner. See you later."
(Carla smiles at both, gets up and leaves.)

Responding provides the basis upon which the helping process is built. It facilitates the helpees' exploration of where they are in relation to their worlds. We listen to the helpees so that we can respond to them. Responding emphasizes entering the helpees' frames of reference and communicating to them what we hear. In other words, there are two separate sets of skills involved: discriminating accurately the dimensions of the helpees' experiences; and communicating accurately to the helpees the dimensions we have perceived.

Responding involves responding to content, feeling and meaning. We respond to content in order to clarify the ingredients of the helpees' experiences. We respond to feeling in order to clarify the affect attached to the experience. We respond to meaning in order to provide the reason for the feeling.

Responding facilitates helpee exploring. When the helper responds accurately to the helpees, then the helpees explore where they are in relation to their worlds. Responding both stimulates and reinforces helpee exploring. It lays the base for personalizing to facilitate helpee understanding.

RESPONDING FACILITATES HELPEE EXPLORING

Another word for responding accurately is empathy. Empathy is a word we use when we crawl inside another person's skin and see the world through his or her eyes. We communicate empathy when we respond interchangeably with the expressions of another person. The First Americans used to speak of "walking in another's moccasins".

In order to be fully responsive with our helpees, there are several helping behaviors we must demonstrate. First of all, we must continue to suspend our own frames of reference. We communicate unconditional regard for the helpees' frames of reference by suspending our own. In this way, the helpees can experience a freedom to explore themselves without fear of retaliation.

Secondly, we must communicate in a genuine manner but we must not share our experiences in any way that may be overwhelming for the helpees. Rather we must emphasize presenting no phoniness or facade that would misrepresent us and make the helpees uncomfortable and unable to share themselves.

Thirdly, we must emphasize specificity in exploring content. The more specific the helpees are about their experiences, the more emphatic the helper can be. Specificity leads directly to responding to content.

THE CORE CONDITIONS OF EXPLORING

PHASE I OF HELPING

HELPER DIMENSIONS	SKILLS LEVEL EMPHASIS
Empathy	Responding Interchangeably
Respect	Communicating Unconditional Regard
Genuineness	Presenting No Facade
Concreteness	Dealing with Specific Experiences
	↓
HELPEE PROCESS	EXPLORING

PHASE I CORE HELPING SKILLS

Responding to Content

We respond first to the most obvious part of the helpees' expressions — the content. We respond to content in order to clarify the critical ingredients of the helpees' experiences. Having an accurate content data base enables us to establish our responsive base in helping: responding to feeling and meaning. In turn, the responsive base enables us to personalize understanding and initiate acting.

The ingredients of content emphasize the basic interrogatives which may be summarized as 5WH: who, what, why, when, where and how. The ingredients of content also emphasize the ordering, importance and cause-effect relationship of the events.

A good response rephrases the helpees' expressions in a fresh way. It does not simply "parrot" back the helpees' own words. A good format for responding to content is:

"You're saying _____."

or

"In other words, _____."

> *"You're saying that since your child lost his innocence, you can never feel the same about him again."*

LISTENING ➡ RESPONDING TO CONTENT

The basic interrogatives provide us with a format for testing the completeness of the helpees' expressions of their experiences. In other words, they enable us to determine whether the helpees have included everything we need to know. The interrogatives may be formulated as follows:

Who and *what* was involved?
What did they do?
Why and *how* did they do it?
When and *where* did they do it?
How well did they do it?

For example, in responding to content, we may examine the following expression for the interrogatives:

"I thought I had things together with my teacher."
Who

"But now I flunked the exam."
What

"I guess we were on different wavelengths."
Why and How

"I guess I didn't study enough at home."
Where and When

"I sure didn't expect questions that hard."
How Well

"In other words, you overestimated where you were with the teacher and with your subject."

RESPONDING TO COMPLETE EXPRESSIONS

There are three basic ways we can organize the helpees' expressions of content. First, we can organize the expressions chronologically. Chronological order means the order in which the events occurred.

The following is a good format for chronologically responding to content:

"You're saying that what happened to you is _____
1st event

followed by _____ and finally _____."
2nd event   3rd event

Thus, for example, we may respond chronologically to a distraught college student in the following manner:

"You're saying that you had a blow-up with your girl and then your folks and finally you flunked your final exams."

"Then you flunked your exam."
3rd event

"Then you had a fight with your folks."
2nd event

"You're saying you had a fight with your girlfriend."
1st event

RESPONDING CHRONOLOGICALLY

The second basic way of organizing the helpees' expressions involves responding to the content in terms of its importance. This means organizing the content from the most important to the least important expression. The following is a good format for responding to importance:
   "You're saying _____ followed by _____
                    most important   *moderately important*
and finally by _____."
              least important
   For example, we may respond to the importance with an addicted person as follows:
   "You're saying that you have a drug problem, and it has had an impact upon your family and your job."

"It also has an impact upon your job."
Least important

"It has an impact upon your family."
Moderately important

"You're saying that you have a drug problem."
Most important

RESPONDING TO IMPORTANCE

The third basic way of organizing helpees' expressions involves responding to content in terms of cause-and-effect relationships. This means identifying how one event or action resulted in the occurrence of another event or action.

The following is a good format for responding to cause-effect relationships:

"You're saying that when _____ then _____."

causal event   effect event

For example, we may respond to a deteriorating marital situation as follows:

"You're saying that since you failed in business, things have never been the same in your marriage."

"This has caused problems in your marriage."
Effect

"You're saying that you failed in business."
Cause

RESPONDING TO CAUSE-EFFECT EVENTS

Responding to the content facilitates the helpees' exploring of any "gaps" in the content. If any of the interrogative questions are unanswered, we may probe them to get a more complete picture of the helpees' experiences. The presence of all of these essential ingredients will enable us later to diagnose the helpees' deficits in any one or more of these areas. In addition, using one or more of the ways of organizing the content will insure an essential interchangeability of understanding of the content for both helper and helpees. We may wish to practice responding to content in real life or in recorded expressions. Again, the case studies may be helpful material for practicing formulating content responses.

FACILITATING EXPLORING OF CONTENT

Responding to Feeling

Just as we showed our empathy for the helpees by responding to the content of their expressions, we may also show our understanding of their experiences by responding to the feelings which they express. Indeed, responding to content prepares us to respond to the feelings of the helpees' expressions. Responding to feelings is the most critical single skill in helping because it reflects the helpees' affective experience of themselves relative to their worlds.

Helpees may express verbally and directly those feelings which dominate them. Or the helpees may only express their feelings indirectly through their tone of voice or by describing the situation in which they find themselves.

Whether the helpees' expressions are direct or indirect, our goal as helpers will be to explicitly show the helpees our level of understanding of their feelings. This will give the helpees a chance to check out our effectiveness as helpers. It will also give us a chance to check ourselves out.

Responding to feelings involves asking and answering the empathy question and developing interchangeable responses to feelings.

RESPONDING TO
CONTENT RESPONDING TO
FEELING

To respond to the helpees' feelings, we must do several things. First, as we have learned, we must observe their behaviors. In particular, we must pay attention to the helpees' postural and facial expressions. The helpees' self-expressions will tell us a great deal about how they experience themselves. Their tones of voice and facial expressions will be valuable clues to their inner feelings.

Next, we must listen carefully to the helpees' words. When we have listened to the words, we must summarize what we have seen and heard that indicates the helpees' feelings. Then we ask ourselves the question, "If I were the helpee and I were doing and saying these things, how would I feel?" In answering this question, you can first identify the general feeling category (happy, angry, sad, surprised, scared, distressed, relieved or calm) and the intensity of the feeling (high, medium or low). Then select a feeling word or phrase that fits the feeling area and level of intensity. Finally, check out the feeling expression with your observations to see if it is appropriate for the helpees involved. (For example, it would not be appropriate to use the word "morose" to capture the feeling of gloom of a helpee with a sixth-grade education.)

*"How would I feel
if I were the helpee?"*

ASKING THE EMPATHY QUESTION

Now we can try to understand the feelings expressed by our helpee. Summarize the clues to the helpee's feelings and then answer the question "How would I feel if I were he and saying these things?"

> *"Things are not going so good for me. Not in school. Not with my girl. I just seem to be floundering. I fake it every day but inside I'm really down because I'm not sure of what I want to do or where I want to go."*

The main cue to the helpee's feeling is that he says he feels down. He's down about school and down about his relationship with his girl. He's also floundering. If we were in his position, we might very well feel sad.

Practice asking and answering to yourself the "How would I feel?" question with other expressions that you hear in everyday life.

"I'd feel sad if I were he!"

ANSWERING THE EMPATHY QUESTION

We can insure that we respond to the helpees' feelings
when we make a response that is interchangeable with
the feelings expressed. It certainly is not too much to expect that we be able to communicate to the helpees what
they have communicated to us. Understanding what the
helpees have expressed—at the level they have expressed it—constitutes the only basis for helping.

A response is interchangeable if both the helper and
the helpee express the same feeling. Operationally, in
terms of the feelings expressed, the helper could have
said what the helpee said.

The first response which we formulate should involve
very simple feeling words reflecting the feelings expressed by the helpee. We may do this by using a simple
"You feel _____" formulation. Before we move to
more complex communication, we must learn to formulate simple responses.

"You feel _____"

DEVELOPING INTERCHANGEABLE RESPONSES

We may say that we respond to the helpees' feelings when we capture the essence of their feelings in one or more feeling words. To capture their feelings, then, we need to know a lot of feeling words. We need to develop a feeling-word vocabulary. It is not enough to understand what the helpees are saying. We must also communicate to the helpees our understanding of their feelings.

DEVELOPING FEELING WORDS

Now let us try to formulate a feeling response to the helpee's expression. Let us repeat Tom's expression again:

"Things are not going so good for me. Not in school. Not with my girl. I just seem to be floundering. I fake it every day but inside I'm really down because I'm not sure of what I want to do or where I want to go."

Again, we have asked ourselves, "How would I feel if I were he?" We answer, "Sad—I would feel sad." Now we formulate the response in a way that we can communicate directly how he feels: "You feel sad."

RESPONDING TO SAD FEELINGS

As you have found, the helpees exhibit many different moods—many different feeling states. Sometimes they seem very sad. Sometimes they seem very happy. Sometimes they seem very angry. Most times they are somewhere in between these extremes.

We must have responses which communicate to them our understanding in each of these moments. Formulate simple responses to each of the helpees' feeling states.

One of the feelings that seems to dominate our helpee is a kind of sad or "down" feeling. His energy level appears low. Things seem pretty hopeless. He feels helpless in the face of everything. He just does not know where he is going or whether he can get there. Sometimes he verbalizes this feeling: "Sometimes I just think that I'm not going to make it."

Using the appropriate feeling word for this kind of sadness, we might formulate a simple response.

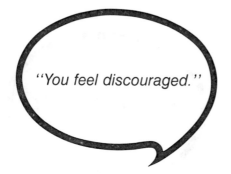

"You feel discouraged."

RESPONDING ACCURATELY

In rare moments, our helpees might be "up," particularly when they have found some direction—however tentative. Their whole demeanor changes. Their attitude toward life opens up. Their behavior is intense and rapid.

It is just as important to be able to respond to the helpees in these moments as it is to respond to them in their depressed moments. Indeed, it is ultimately more important.

While it is critical to pick our helpees up at the level that they are expressing themselves, we must ultimately help them to move to new and more rewarding behavior. We cannot help them to move if we cannot respond to those rare moments of joy.

For many of us, these are the most difficult experiences to respond to. Sharing another's joy is difficult indeed for those of us whose own moments of joy are few and far between.

Sometimes our helpee's feelings are so intense that he blurts them out: "I can't wait to get started!"

We might formulate a simple response to Tom's feeling state.

RESPONDING TO HAPPY FEELINGS

At times, the helpees might express other kinds of feelings which might be difficult to respond to. Sometimes they are just mad at the world, angry with its injustice and motivated to retaliate. Their bodies are tense, their eyes tearing and their expressions choked. Often we are afraid to open up such feelings. We are afraid of how far these feelings may carry them. "Will they act upon them?" "Will they act them out?" These are the questions which characterize our concern.

Nevertheless, we cannot help if we cannot deal with all of a person's feelings. Our helpee must get these feelings out in the open if he is going to learn to deal with them. Indeed, the probability of his acting upon angry feelings is inversely related to his ability to explore them. The more he explores them, the less likely he is to act destructively. Put another way, the more he explores them, the more likely he is to channel them constructively. Sometimes he expresses his feelings in violent terms: "I know damn well I'm going to get back at him any way I can."

We may formulate a simple response to him.

"You feel furious."

RESPONDING TO ANGRY FEELINGS

We must respond to our helpees in all their fullness—in their moments of sadness, happiness and anger. They are how they feel.

If we do not respond to our helpees in their fullness, the implications are clear: if we cannot find them, we lose them. If we lose them, they cannot find themselves.

There are many unique feeling words that could be used to capture our helpees' experiences. We may practice formulating at least 10 feeling words each for the feeling states of sadness, happiness and anger. Let us see if we can determine what kinds of helpee expressions might call for using any one of these words.

Sad
Distressed
Down
Lousy
Bad

     Happy
     Excited
     Elated
     Up
     Good

          Angry
          Annoyed
          Furious
          Irritated
          Mad

RESPONDING TO UNIQUE FEELINGS

In addition, there are many variations of these feeling themes. Other major themes are surprise, fright, relief, distress, affection, disgust, interest and shame. There is a wide range of feeling states to which we can respond.

We must learn to respond to these unique feelings. It is beneficial for both the helpers and the helpees to struggle to capture in words the uniqueness of the helpees' experiences.

When our helpee has lost his direction and expresses himself in this manner—"I just don't know which way to turn"—we might respond to his loss of direction. We may try formulating a number of words which capture the uniqueness of his experience.

"You feel lost."

RESPONDING TO OTHER FEELINGS

The more feeling words we have available, the better our chances of matching the words with our helpees' unique experiences.

When our helpee finds himself in a situation where he feels his insides tugged and offers "I feel like I am getting pulled both ways," we might respond to his inner struggle.

One effective way of organizing feeling words is to categorize them according to whether they are of high, medium or low intensity. Since the intensity of any word depends upon the person with whom it is used, we will need to visualize the typical helpees we work with to categorize by intensity level. Then we can discriminate both the feeling category and the level of intensity which we wish to employ. We may develop our own word list by filling in the next two pages. Appendix A contains an alphabetical listing of feeling words from which to draw. We may carry the list around with us and add to it. It will help us respond accurately.

"You feel torn."

THE MORE FEELING WORDS WE KNOW . . .

Categories of Feelings

Levels of Intensity	Excited	Surprised	Happy	Satisfied	Appreciative	Affectionate	Relieved	Calm
High	Delirious Intoxicated Exhilarated	Astonished Staggered Stupefied	Ecstatic Exuberant Triumphant	Delighted Enchanted Satiated	Cherish Revere Treasure	Love Infatuated Rapture	Consoled Freed Solaced	Pacified Sedated Serene
Medium	Animated Charged Thrilled	Amazed Awed Jolted	Exalted Fantastic Tickled	Charmed Gratified Full	Adore Esteem Prize	Affectionate Revered Endeared	Allayed Comforted Unburdened	Collected Mellow Restful
Low	Alive Great Stirred	Overcome Rocked Startled	Great Lively Super	Agreeable Glad Nice	Admire Regard Value	Close Like Warm	At ease Helped Rested	Bland Quiet Undisturbed

. . . The Easier It Will Be to Respond Accuratey

Categories of Feelings

Levels of Intensity	Distressed	Frightened	Anxious	Sad	Angry	Disgusted	Ashamed	Embarrassed
High	Agony Crushed Tormented	Frantic Terrified Petrified	Baffled Perplexed Tangled	Despair Devastated Pitiful	Enraged Infuriated Livid	Abhorred Abominated Repugnant	Humiliated Mortified Sinful	Demeaned Flustered Stupid
Medium	Afflicted Pained Troubled	Aghast Dread Threatened	Blocked Confounded Stressed	Awful Gloomy Sullen	Bristle Fuming Indignant	Evil Nauseated Vile	Chagrined Criminal Derelict	Disconcerted Dumb Rattled
Low	Bad Ill at ease Upset	Cautious Hesitant Shakey	Careful Muddled Uncertain	Down Low Unhappy	Annoyed Crabby Sore	Averse Gross Rotten	Contrite Regretful Shame	Awkward Foolish Silly

. . . So That We Can Encourage Helpee Exploration

Perhaps we have had some difficulty coming up with feeling words that are interchangeable with our helpee's feelings. Remember, always return to our observations for explicit cues to actual helpee feelings.

If we can't find the "right" word, but we know we are in the "ball park", try this technique. We may simply ask ourselves "When I feel _____ how do I
                        general feeling
feel?" For instance, if the helpee says "I feel helpless," and we find ourselves at a loss for a new word with which to respond, we ask ourselves "How do I feel when I feel helpless?"

We might answer, "Scared." Look at the helpee—does the helpee feel scared? If not, we repeat the question—only this time using "scared" as the stimulus. "How do I feel if I feel scared?" We might say, "I feel trapped." We continue to recycle the question and check out the new feeling words with our observations of the helpee until we have an interchangeable feeling word.

Again, we may wish to practice responding to feelings in life or recordings. The case studies may provide helpful stimulus materials for formulating feeling responses.

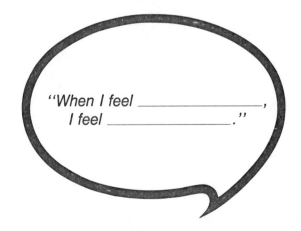

*"When I feel _____,
I feel _____."*

FACILITATING EXPLORING OF FEELING

Responding to Meaning

Responding separately to the feeling or the content of the helpees' expressions is not enough. Our response must be enriched by putting the feeling together with the content for the helpees.

Content is used to make the feeling meaningful. The content gives intellectual meaning to the helpees' expressions of their experiences. The feeling gives emotional meaning to the helpees' expressions of their experiences. Responding to meaning emphasizes making interchangeable responses that capture both the feeling and content of the expressions.

RESPONDING TO   ➡   RESPONDING TO
FEELING   MEANING

Remember, feelings are about content. The content provides the reason for the feeling. For example, let us look at several feeling states and the related content areas.

Feeling	Content
Happy	about being promoted
Angry	with my teacher for giving me a low grade
Sad	when I knew that I'd never see her again

We may practice responding to meaning by supplying the content of different feeling responses in our own lives as well as others.

"She feels upset about her family."

FEELINGS ABOUT CONTENT

A response to meaning is not complete until it communicates both feeling and content. A helpful response complements feeling with content. Understanding of the helpees' expressions can be communicated by complementing a response to feeling with a response to content. For example, whereas "You're saying that _____" expressed the content of the helpee's expression and "You feel _____" expressed the helpee's feelings, "You feel _____ because _____" captures both the feeling and the content. This is an effective format for a complete interchangeable response to the helpee.

"You feel _____ because _____."

RESPONDING INTERCHANGEABLY

It is as if we try to understand with our minds what the helpees feel in their guts. We do this first by crawling inside of their feelings. We do this second by comprehending the content of their expressions.

Whereas "You feel sad" expressed the helpee's feelings with the passing of a loved one, "You feel sad because she was the most important person in the world to you and now she is gone" captures the meaning in the feeling and the content.

CAPTURING BOTH THE FEELING AND THE CONTENT

If we do not respond to the content of the helpees' expressions, we will often find ourselves unable to work with their problems. Things that we can frame in our minds are easier to do something about than those which we only feel. If we do not respond to the content and the feeling, we will not be able to bring the helping process to an action stage. We will have failed the helpees and they, in turn, will fail.

Let us spend another moment with our helpee. He is angry and states, "I am just so angry at them. First they give me the opportunity and then they take it away." Let us formulate a response that reflects both the feeling and content expressed by Tom.

Sometimes the helpees express multiple feelings and content. It is important for us to attend to all of the major feelings and contents.

Now our helpee is saying a lot more than that he is angry. If your response to his initial expression was effective, he might add "Now it's gone and I won't ever get it again." Let us formulate a response that captures the feeling and content of his new expression.

"You felt furious because they cheated you out of a real chance and now you feel sad because the opportunity is lost."

RESPONDING TO MANY FEELINGS AND CONTENTS

If we respond accurately to our helpees' expressions, we will involve them in exploring themselves in the areas in which they are having difficulty. Because we have understood Tom accurately at the level that he has presented himself, he will go on to share many other personal experiences of this and other situations.

He will also bring his friends around because we are good helpers. It is time to meet some of these friends. One is Joan—a cautious young woman. As a young person growing into adulthood, she is increasingly aware of the differences in her experiences from young men. She is also increasingly aware of the conflict arising out of her desires for a professional career.

While we attend to Joan, she is reserved. She looks us over carefully. We might formulate an effective response.

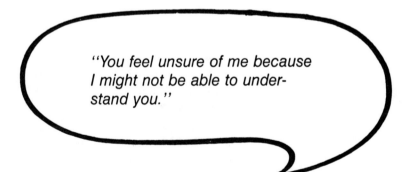

"You feel unsure of me because I might not be able to understand you."

RESPONDING TO DIFFICULT FEELINGS AND CONTENTS

There are as many responses as there are people. As helpers, we must learn to attend to all of these people and to break free of our own restrictive experiences to enter their worlds and individualize our responses.

Another of our helpee's friends is Floyd—an expressive young man. Floyd is black. Just as being a woman makes a difference in experience, so does being black, as does anything that makes us stand out. Floyd is assertive in expressing this: "I don't need this stuff. You can never know what it is like to be me!" We might formulate an effective response to Floyd's expression.

The important thing is not what words we employ, but how we enter the helpees' frames of reference to understand the feeling and content which they have expressed. How we communicate that understanding at the level that they have expressed their concerns is also important.

Joan may acknowledge the possibility that we might help her, but she is going to be cautious before involving herself. Floyd may acknowledge that we can help him but only if we acknowledge that there may be limits to the depth of our understanding.

Indeed, we may respond to each as part of a group. We may communicate to each our understanding of his or her frame of reference. We may also facilitate each person's understanding of the others' frames of reference.

We should continue to practice responding to other people whom we meet in our daily living. As we practice, our own skill level will increase and we will be better prepared to enter the frames of reference of others. Again, we can use the case studies as well as live interactions for practicing.

"You feel doubtful because I can't ever really know your experience."

FACILITATING EXPLORING OF MEANING

Summary

One way of structuring responding is to test the comprehensiveness and accuracy of our responses to the helpees' expressions. We may simply attend, observe and listen to the next expression we hear. Let us rate our accuracy of responding to the helpee's experience as follows:

High responsiveness — Accurate interchangeable response to feeling and content

Moderate responsiveness — Accurate interchangeable response to feeling

Low responsiveness — Accurate interchangeable response to content

As can be seen, the low levels of responsiveness are consistent with the high levels of attentiveness (listening and repeating verbatim). The moderate levels of responsiveness involve responding to both feeling and content.

LEVELS OF RESPONDING

Now we can continue to build our own cumulative rating scale for helping. If the helper is attentive and responsive to meaning (feeling and content) we can rate the helper at a fully-responsive level (level 3.0). If the helper responds to feeling alone, we can rate the helper at a partially-responsive level (level 2.5). If the helper is observing and listening but responding to only the content of the helpees' expressions, we can rate the helper at less than a facilitative level (level 2.0).

LEVELS OF HELPING

5.0	
4.5	
4.0	
3.5	
3.0	**Responding to meaning**
2.5	**Responding to feeling**
2.0	**Responding to content**
	(observing and listening)
1.5	**Attending personally**
1.0	**Nonattending**

LEVELS OF HELPING: ATTENDING AND RESPONDING

Again, the function of responding to the helpees' experiences is to facilitate their self-exploration of areas of concern. The areas explored by the helpees should be accompanied by feelings that are appropriate to the material being explored. Our awareness of the goals of exploring feeling and content will enable us to reinforce those helpee behaviors that accomplish the goals.

When the helpees become able to explore themselves at levels interchangeable with those expressed, the helpees signal a readiness for the next goal of helping—understanding. As helpers, we understand that there is no value to exploration unless it facilitates an understanding that goes beyond the material presented. Helpees must explore where they are in order to understand where they want to be. The helpees' readiness for understanding signals helpers to begin personalizing.

PHASES OF HELPING

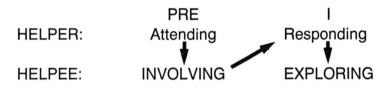

FACILITATING INVOLVING AND EXPLORING

You now know something about attending and responding skills. You will want to continue practicing these skills until you have integrated them into your helping personality. Practice using these skills in the following case study.

Case Study #4—Skilled Responding

Carol Lewis is a 34-year-old woman. She is the mother of three children, a set of identical twin 4-year-old boys, Adam and Aaron, and a 6-year-old daughter, Nancy. Carol was widowed when her husband, Mark, died of a malignant brain tumor.

During his last few weeks, Mark was in a hospital. The last four days he was in a coma. Carol stayed at the hospital with him the last five days of his life, leaving the children with her parents.

The Lewis' were assigned to David Biloxi, a hospital social worker. Following is an excerpt of a conversation between David and Carol the day before Mark died. The conversation took place in a private lounge on Mark's ward.

David: "Let's sit down here." (gestures to the couch). "Would you like some juice or something to eat?"

Carol: (sitting down) "No, I'm not hungry."

David: "You're looking pretty tired."

Carol: "I just haven't been able to sleep much."

David: "This is really a difficult time for you."

Carol: "I'm still not able to believe it's happening. I mean, a month ago we were planning to buy a new house. Mark had just gotten a promotion. And now, any minute he'll be. . .he'll be. . .gone. Dead."

David: "The whole thing is still unreal. A few weeks ago, the two of you were planning for the future together. Now, Mark is dying."

Carol: "It's so unbelievably unfair!" (shaking her head and clenching her fist).

David: "You're really angry about it all."

Carol: "I'm so damn mad! Damn mad! God...I just don't understand."

David: "You're furious because of the unjustness of Mark's death."

Carol: "And the worst part is I'm so angry with God and the doctors and everybody."

David: "You're so enraged by what's happening that everyone becomes a target."

Carol: "Yes. And the horrible thing is..." (she starts to cry) "I'm so angry with Mark for leaving me. Sometimes I don't know if I can forgive him."

David: "You're especially angry with Mark because he's leaving you, abandoning you."

Carol: (crying harder) "That's right. I just don't know what I'll do without him...I love him so much...Mark...Mark...Oh God!"

David: (taking Carol into his arms and holding her as she sobs) "It really hurts having him die because of how much he means to you."

Carol: "He's been my life...even more than the children. With him gone, everything will be so empty. I'll be so...alone."

David: "You're frightened because you're going to be alone, having to live without Mark."

Carol: "That's it! That's why I'm so angry. I'm scared of being left alone. How could he do this to me!"

David: "You're frightened because you have to start over."

4
Personalizing —
Facilitating Helpee
Understanding

It is a short step from the children's becoming aware of the ingredients of human experience to anticipating particular experiences. With the increasing confidence brought about by an awareness of the relationship of stimulus and response, the children are prepared for purposeful learning at about a year of age. At this point, the children can set out to obtain a certain result or end, independent of the means employed. For example, the children may set out to attract their parents or obtain food or objects that are out of reach.

Drawing from this awareness of the relationship between stimulus and response or cause and effect, the children set goals of achieving certain effects. The goals of their instrumental acts are often only seen later, although some approximation of these goals was obviously intended from the beginning.

The children begin to understand the relationship of their acts to future events or experiences. They are, in effect, attempting to predict the consequences of their efforts. They understand where they want to be in their worlds. This is the beginning of the second stage or phase of human learning. It is what allows humankind to anticipate its future.

Here are some questions that you can ask as you begin to think about personalizing:

How do you know when people have shown that they truly understand the significance of an important experience in your life?

How do you know when someone has correctly inferred something from what you have said?

How do you know when someone has helped you identify problems and goals in your life?

Case Study #5—Unskilled Personalizing

Bill Huachuca is a 21-year-old student. He is a journalism major with one more year of schooling to complete. For the last 18 months he has been seeing the same woman, Lisa, a 19-year-old medical technician major.

Bill came to the school's counseling center because Lisa had told Bill that she didn't want to see him anymore. She wanted to be free to "party". Bill subsequently tried to talk with Lisa who told him that she found him to be "lazy, boring, dull" and not to call her again. Bill became depressed and sought help after he had gone out with a friend, gotten drunk, and spent the rest of the night crying and shouting things like, "Lisa don't leave me, I love you!"

Bill has been seeing Tom Travis, a counseling intern working at the center. The following excerpt is from their second session together.

Bill: "I just can't get Lisa off my mind. I can't study. I can't work. I don't eat or sleep. All I do is think of Lisa! Lisa!"

Tom: "You're saying that your relationship with Lisa is the only thing you can focus on right now."

Bill: "Right, I can't stand being without her. I don't know if I can make it without her."

Tom: "You're really feeling scared because she's left you."

Bill: "I wish I knew what I did wrong!"

Tom: "You're angry with yourself because you couldn't keep her."

Bill: "She thinks I'm a bore, that I'm dull. She doesn't believe I have anything to offer."

Tom: "You're feeling guilty because she doesn't find you exciting."

Bill: "I guess I am a little dull. I mean I really live a quiet kind of life."

Tom: "You're saying you see your life as quiet and can understand how that might be dull for Lisa."

Bill: "Yeah, she wants to go out partying and drinking. She likes crowds and dancing and all that kind of stuff. I just don't enjoy it. I'd rather be home relaxing. I need my privacy."

Tom: "You're saying that you and Lisa want to do different kinds of things."

Bill: "I just don't know how to be the kind of person she wants to be with. I wish I did."

Tom: "You feel discouraged because you don't know how to be the kind of person Lisa wants."

Bill: "It's more than that, I guess; but I'm not sure what."

Tom: "You're saying there is more to your discouragement than not being able to meet Lisa's expectations."

Bill: "Yeah, I got a feeling that I wasn't, well . . . as exciting a lover as she wanted."

Tom: "You're saying you're unsure about yourself as a lover."

Bill: "Right, I don't know if I've got what it takes to, you know, turn women on."

Tom: "You're feeling scared because you don't know if you're exciting enough."

Bill: "Yeah, right! And I can't do anything about it. I'm a dull person and a lousy lover. Maybe I should become a priest or something."

Tom: "You feel discouraged and embarrassed because you can't change the way you are."

Bill: "Maybe Lisa is right about leaving me."

Tom: "You're saying you understand why Lisa left you."

Bill: "I just don't think I'll ever be any different."

Tom: "You feel disgusted because you don't think you can be any different."

Bill: "Do you know of any superstud pills I could take?"

Tom: "Well, no, I don't, Bill. But I think we're really making progress here. You're saying some really personal things and they're very important. I'm sure if we keep on talking we'll get somewhere."

Bill: "Well, okay, but we've been through this all before."

Tom: "You're saying we're covering the same ground again and that's right. But we're talking about these things a little differently. I think we're getting to some kind of understanding."

Bill: "Maybe you're right."

Personalizing is the most critical dimension for human change or gain. Personalizing is so critical because it emphasizes internalizing the helpees' responsibilities for the helpees' problems. It involves going beyond the material expressed by the helpees. When we add accurately to the expressions of the helpees, we are facilitating their understanding of where they are in relation to where they want or need to be.

Personalizing involves personalizing the meaning or the implications of the response to meaning. Personalizing emphasizes internalizing the responsibility for the helpees' response deficits. Personalizing leads directly to the goal implied by the deficit. Personalizing also involves recycling the new feelings attendant to the personalized meaning, problems and goals. Personalizing facilitates helpee understanding and prepares us for initiating helpee action.

PERSONALIZING FACILITATES
HELPEE UNDERSTANDING

Before we can move on to personalizing, we must establish a base of communication. Responding interchangeably to the helpees' expressions insures that we understand each of the helpees' expressions at the level presented. When we have made responses that incorporate accurately the feeling and meaning expressed by the helpees, we say that we have established an interchangeable base of communication.

In building an interchangeable base of communication, we may find it expedient to ask questions to fill certain "gaps" in our understanding. When we ask a question, we should follow it with a response. Indeed, the test of a good question is whether we can respond accurately to the helpees' answers. The skilled helper will sandwich questions between two interchangeable responses. Of course, if we find ourselves asking two consecutive questions without responding, then in all probability we have asked bad questions and should return to responding accurately.

In building an interchangeable base of communication, the helpees will inform us directly through their behaviors of their readiness to move on to additive levels. They alert us by demonstrating their ability to sustain self-exploratory behavior and to respond accurately to their own expressions. In other words, the helpees inform us of their readiness for movement to the next level by doing for themselves the things that we have been doing for them.

BUILDING AN INTERCHANGEABLE
BASE OF COMMUNICATION

As we move toward personalizing, we are becoming increasingly additive in our empathic responsiveness. In practice, this means that we use the interchangeable base of communication to go beyond what the helpees have said. We use the meaning of the helpees' expressions to consider, increasingly, the personal implications for the helpees.

In terms of the respect dimension, we communicate increasingly positive regard for the assets the helpees have demonstrated. This will serve to reinforce the constructive behaviors of the helpees. In relating, we will become increasingly genuine. As we come to know the helpees, we can share ourselves tentatively, studying the feedback we get from the helpees for cues about the effects of our sharing. In terms of concreteness, we become more specific as we increasingly search to define the helpees' problems and goals.

THE CORE CONDITIONS OF UNDERSTANDING

PHASE II OF HELPING

HELPER DIMENSIONS	SKILLS LEVEL EMPHASIS
Empathy	Personalizing Empathic Responses
Respect	Communicating Positive Regard
Genuineness	Becoming Genuine
Concreteness	Concretizing Problems

	↓
HELPEE PROCESS	UNDERSTANDING

PHASE II CORE HELPING SKILLS

Personalizing Meaning

Personalizing meaning is the first step toward facilitating the helpees' understanding of where they are in relation to where they want or need to be. We personalize the meaning when we relate the meaning directly to the helpees' experiences. In other words, we zero in on why the experiences are significant for the helpees.

In responding to meaning, we answered the question, "What is the situation and how do the helpees feel about it?" Now we answer the question, "What is the effect of the situation upon the helpees?"

Personalizing the meaning involves personalizing common themes, internalizing experiences and personalizing implications. The common themes provide the basis for making personalized responses. Internalizing experience emphasizes making the helpees accountable for their experiences. Personalizing implications emphasizes developing the personal implications for the helpees.

RESPONDING TO ⟶ PERSONALIZING
MEANING   MEANING

Personalized responses are always formulated from the helpees' frames of reference. They acknowledge the helpees' experiences of the world and build upon those experiences. Just as we formulated personalized meaning responses to individual helpee expressions, we also formulate personalized meaning responses to the helpees' expressions made over a period of time.

We do this by looking for the common themes in the helpees' expressions. The themes relate to what the helpees are saying about themselves. The common themes are derived from the extended base of communication. They are those themes which are interwoven through more than one of the helpees' expressions. When one common theme stands out above others because of recurrence or intensity, we may call it a dominant theme. In responding to the common or dominant theme, we may use the format:

"You feel _____ because things are always _____."

"You feel furious because things are always interfering."

PERSONALIZING COMMON THEMES

The common themes may be personalized by internalizing the helpees' experiences. So often we find that helpees are talking about third persons—other friends, students, teachers, spouses, parents, children—about whom we can do nothing directly. By concentrating upon others, the helpees are externalizing their experiences. By internalizing their experiences, we concentrate upon the helpees.

In responding to meaning, we used the format, "You feel _____ because _____." Now we internalize the meaning by introducing the helpees into the response: "You feel _____ because you _____." For example, we may internalize our experiences concerning breakdowns in communication with others, or in learning with our teachers or in performance on our jobs. When our helpee expressed his experience of his lost opportunity, we may have responded: "You feel furious because they cheated you out of a real chance." Now we may internalize the meaning by internalizing the experience for the helpee.

"You feel furious because you got cheated."

INTERNALIZING EXPERIENCES

The key ingredient in personalizing meaning is considering the personal implications for the helpees. We do this by asking why the experience is important for the helpees. Put another way, we ask how their experiences impacted them. We are looking at the consequences of their experiences for the helpees.

In personalizing the meaning, we may use the format, "You feel _____ because you always _____."
Thus, for example, we may personalize the implications for any living, learning and working experience. After asking the personal implications question, we may make a personalized response to our helpee's experience of a lost opportunity.

"You feel furious because you are always getting left behind."

PERSONALIZING IMPLICATIONS

We must continue to check back with the helpees to stay in tune with their experiences. In so doing, we may find that their feelings are changing. For example, realizing he has been left behind, the helpee may find himself feeling more frustrated or upset with himself than furious with other people. If we do not have a precisely-accurate feeling response, we continue to cycle the feeling question: "How does that make me feel?" We may continue to practice personalizing meaning in live or recorded interactions such as the case studies.

"You feel frustrated because you are always getting left behind."

PERSONALIZING FEELINGS ABOUT MEANING

Personalizing Problems

Personalizing problems is the most critical transitional step to action. It is from our problems that we derive our goals. It is from our goals that we derive our action programs.

Personalizing problems is based upon personalizing meaning. We personalize problems when we help the helpees to understand what they cannot do that has led to their personalized experience of themselves. In other words, based upon the personalized meaning of the experience for the helpees, we answer the question of personalized problems: What is there about the helpees that is contributing to the problems? In responding to personalized meaning, we looked at the personal impact of the situation upon the helpees. Now we are asking the helpees to take responsibility for their lives and to look at themselves as the source of their problems. Personalizing problems involves conceptualizing, internalizing and concretizing deficits.

PERSONALIZING ➤ PERSONALIZING
MEANING   PROBLEMS

In conceptualizing the deficits, we ask the question: What was missing that contributed to the problem? The question is asked independently of the source of the problem. It is simply an attempt to ascertain the missing ingredient that might have contributed to the problem. Sometimes we are initially unaware of what that ingredient might be. We might have to search out expert information and people for advice.

For example, a facilitative interpersonal relationship may have been missing in the breakdown of communication with our parents, friends, teachers or employers. In the illustration of our helpee's lost opportunity, some initiative was missing. Perhaps no one took the initiative to make the opportunity clear to him. Certainly, he did not take the initiative to take advantage of the opportunity. We may conceptualize the deficit by using the format: "You feel _____ because _____ was missing."

"*You feel frustrated because initiative was missing.*"

CONCEPTUALIZING DEFICITS

Again, we must internalize the deficits. This means making the helpees accountable or responsible for their roles in the deficits. They must ask and answer the internalizing question: What is there about me that contributed to the problem?

For example, they may discover their roles in the breakdown in communication with parents or friends or in learning with the teachers or in working with the employers. In responding to the internalized deficit for our helpee's lost opportunity, we may internalize the deficit by using the format: "You feel _____ because you cannot _____."

"You feel frustrated because you cannot assume initiative."

INTERNALIZING DEFICITS

Finally, it is important to concretize the deficit. If we can
concretize the deficit, then we will be able to concretize
the goal and, thus, make it achievable. In concretizing the
deficit, we answer the question: How can we observe or
measure the deficit?

For example, in the breakdown of communication, we
may observe or measure the deficit by criteria for a lack
of attentiveness or responsiveness between parties. In
concretizing our helpee's initiative deficit, we may
observe or measure the deficit by an inability to take programmatic steps to take advantage of the opportunity
when it arose. In concretizing deficits, we may use the
format: "You feel _____ because you cannot
_____ as indicated by _____."

> "You feel frustruated because you cannot assume
> initiative as indicated by your inability to take the
> right steps at the right time."

CONCRETIZING DEFICITS

Again, we will want to personalize the new feelings attendant to the personalized problem. Personalizing the feelings emphasizes responding to how the helpees feel about their deficits. Almost universally, helpees' experiences evolve to "down" feelings or feelings of sadness. As we continue to ask the feeling question, "How does that make me feel?", we usually end up with feelings involving disappointment. Thus, for example, feelings of pain or hurt or weakness or vulnerability usually become feelings of self-disappointment because the helpees lack the responses to handle their situations. Thus, the helpees feel disappointed in themselves due to the breakdown in communication. Similarly, our helpee feels disappointed because of his lack of initiative.

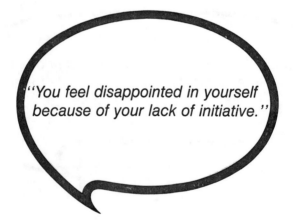

"You feel disappointed in yourself because of your lack of initiative."

PERSONALIZING FEELINGS ABOUT DEFICITS

Sometimes we may choose to expedite personalizing problems through confrontations. Confrontations may take many forms. We may confront the helpees with behaviors that disagree with what they say. Sometimes we point to a discrepancy between how the helpees say they feel and how they appear. A discrepancy might exist between how the helpees really are and how they want to be or how they want to be seen. Or a discrepancy may exist between insight and action.

In making our confrontations, it is usually most effective to use the format for a mild confrontation: "On the one hand, you say/feel/do _____ while on the other hand you say/feel/do _____." When such confrontations are made in the context of a personalized relationship, they may serve to promote open-ended inquiries into the behaviors. An effective confrontation is always followed by an effective helper response. Remember, confrontations are never necessary and never sufficient. However, in the hands of an effective helper, they may be efficient tools to recycle further exploration and understanding.

"You say you feel disappointed in your lack of initiative but you don't do anything about it."

CONFRONTING DEFICITS

Personalizing Goals

Personalizing goals is the simplest transitional step. If we have personalized the problem effectively, then we should be able to personalize the goal fluidly.

Personalizing goals involves establishing where the helpees want to be in relation to where they are. The basic way to personalize goals is to determine the behaviors that are the opposite of the personalized problem. Thus, the goal can be described as the "flip side" of the problem. Personalizing goals involves personalizing, internalizing and concretizing desired or needed assets.

PERSONALIZING ⟶ PERSONALIZING
PROBLEMS   GOALS

Just as we conceptualized the deficits, so do we now conceptualize the desired assets. We simply reverse the question to ask: What might contribute to resolving the problem? Usually, we can find the desired assets by directly reversing the deficits. Thus, an interpersonal deficit implies an interpersonal asset. Similarly, an initiative deficit implies an initiative asset. In conceptualizing assets, you may use the format: "You feel _____ because you cannot _____ and you want to _____."

"You feel disappointed because you cannot initiate and you want to initiate."

CONCEPTUALIZING ASSETS

Sometimes it is still very difficult for the helpees to internalize desired assets. They may understand the logic but are unable to experience themselves with the assets. At this point, it may be necessary to recycle exploring and understanding in order to come to grips with the helpees' potential for learning to develop these assets. Thus, we will want to establish an extensive base of interchangeable responses exploring their inability to internalize potential assets. It may be that we will have to modify our objectives in personalizing goals. When we finally internalize the desired assets, we may use the format: "You feel _____ because _____ and you really want to learn to _____."

"You feel disappointed because you cannot initiate and you really want to learn to initiate."

INTERNALIZING ASSETS

We will want to concretize our potential desired assets just as we concretized our deficits. Again, we may need to search out some sources of expertise in concretizing these assets. Usually, we can reverse the criteria of our concretized deficits. Thus, for example, we may observe our communication assets in terms of criteria of attentiveness and responsiveness. Similarly, with our helpee, we may measure our initiative assets by an ability to take programmatic steps at opportune times. In concretizing assets, we may use the formula: "You feel   because you cannot   and you really want to   as indicated by   "

"You feel disappointed because you cannot initiate and you really want to learn to initiate as indicated by being able to develop and implement initiative programs."

CONCRETIZING ASSETS

Just as we personalized feelings about problems, so do
we personalize feelings about goals. Similarly, just as
"down" feelings are usually attached to problems, so are
"up" feelings or feelings of happiness usually attached to
goals. Thus, the helpees usually become hopeful for their
futures or pleased with having a direction in life. If we
continue to ask the empathy question, "How does that
make me feel?", we may develop feelings of various
degrees of elation, excitement or enthusiasm. In personalizing feelings about goals, we may use the format:
"You feel   because you are going to   ."

*"You feel eager because you are
going to learn to initiate."*

PERSONALIZING FEELINGS ABOUT GOALS

Sometimes the helpees are reluctant to deal with their assets. Depending upon their life experiences, many helpees are more afraid of succeeding than they are of failing. They may be familiar with failing. At some level they may have accommodated failure in their lives with some comfort. If appropriate and expeditious, we may confront strengths as well as weaknesses, assets as well as deficits. In making our confrontations, we may use the format for mild confrontations. We must be sure to respond accurately and extensively to the effects of these confrontations in order to recycle exploring and understanding. Remember, the confrontations are only effective and economical in the hands of a skilled helper.

"You say you are unsure about achieving your goals yet you recognize your strengths in achieving them."

CONFRONTING ASSETS

Let us interact with Floyd as he works through a problem. Formulate interchangeable responses to each of Floyd's expressions. Then formulate a personalized response to meaning. Finally, formulate a response to a personalized problem, feeling and goal.

> "I just don't know what I'm going to do. On one hand, I really want to go. On the other, I don't want to go."

> "Sometimes I'd just like to delay and not decide at all."

> "I guess I just can't make decisions."

> "I guess I really can't fool myself any longer."

> "I'm just going to have to grow up and suffer the consequences."

"You feel disappointed in yourself because of your inability to make mature decisions and you're really committed to learning to do so."

PERSONALIZING UNDERSTANDING

Summary

One way of structuring personalizing is to test the comprehensiveness and accuracy of our personalized response to the helpees' expressions. Let us simply attend and respond in our next encounter. Then we will attempt to rate the accuracy of our personalizing the helpees' experiences as follows:

High personalizing	— Accurately personalized problems, feelings and goals incorporating helpee's response deficit and helpee's response goal
Moderate personalizing	— Accurately personalized meaning incorporating helpee's response deficit and helpee's response goal
Low personalizing	— Accurate responsiveness

As can be seen, the low levels of personalizing are consistent with the high levels of responsiveness (feeling and content). The moderate levels of personalizing involve meaning, while the high levels involve the problems, feelings and goals.

"You're scared because you're not sure you can handle the implications of succeeding—everyone will have high expectancies for your future performance—and you're really enthusiastic about learning how to handle those expectancies."

LEVELS OF PERSONALIZING

We can continue to build our cumulative scale for help-ing. If the helper is attending, responding and personaliz-ing the problem, feelings and goal for the helpee, we can rate the helper at a fully-personalizing level (level 4.0). If the helper is attentive and responsive and personalizes the meaning for the helpee, we can rate the helper at a facilitatively-personalizing level (level 3.5).

LEVELS OF HELPING

5.0	
4.5	
4.0	Personalizing problem, feeling and goal
3.5	Personalizing meaning
3.0	Responding to meaning
2.5	Responding to feeling
2.0	Responding to content
1.5	Attending
1.0	Nonattending

LEVELS OF HELPING:
ATTENDING, RESPONDING AND PERSONALIZING

Formulating an effective personalized response is the key to helping. If we can enter the helpees' frames of reference and enable them to see things clearly, we will help them take the major steps in changing their behaviors. If we cannot do so, the helpees will not have the perspective necessary for developing directions that lead out of their difficulty.

We can test the effectiveness of our personalized responses by interacting with associates. The effectiveness of our formulations may be determined by how well the helpees utilize our personalized attempts. We might try to replicate some of the exercises in this book, then try other kinds of less intense experiences before attempting to use our skills in intense helping situations.

Again, the key to formulating effective personalized responses is discipline. Discipline in building an interchangeable base. Discipline in using that base to search out the common or dominant themes.

As we move to personalized levels of responding, we are, as we have seen, automatically introducing our own experience. That is, we are going beyond what the helpees have expressed. In order to do this, we must be drawing from our own experience.

PHASES OF HELPING

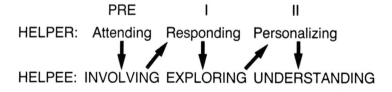

INVOLVING, EXPLORING AND UNDERSTANDING

You now know about attending, responding and personalizing skills. You will need to work most intensely on your personalizing skills because they are most difficult to learn. Practice until you can process these responses easily as in the following case study.

Case Study #6—Skilled Personalizing

Barbara Dix is a 25-year-old graduate student who will complete her masters degree in physics next semester. However, in the last few months she has become unsure of her desire to be a physicist. She already has several job offers when she graduates but has deferred making a decision.

She has sought help from Debbie, an old roommate and friend who is now working in the University's placement office. The following excerpt takes place after two previous sessions and well into the third session.

Barb: "When I realized that the reason I went on with school was to prove to my family that I could do it, I also realized that being a physicist might not be what I really want to do."

Debbie: "You went on to get your masters to prove yourself to your family and now you're not sure if that's what you really want to do."

Barb: "I get so upset with the way they discount me because I'm a girl. They always put my brothers first."

Debbie: "You feel angry because they have never accepted you as an equal to your brothers."

Barb: "The entire thing is just so stupid! I keep trying to prove to them I'm worthy, and no matter what I do they'll never accept me."

Debbie: "You feel disgusted because they can't recognize what you can do."

Barb: "Yes. Why can't I be satisfied with me knowing what I can do?"

Debbie: "You're angry because you haven't been able to break free from wanting to earn their approval."

Barb: "That's right! I can't be satisfied with myself or what I do because I want their respect."

Debbie: "You feel disgusted with yourself because you have let your need for their respect determine what you do with your life."

Barb: "And now at twenty-five, three months away from a masters in physics, I'm not sure if I really want to be a physicist or if I'm doing it solely to earn their love."

Debbie: "You feel scared because you cannot be sure that becoming a physicist is something you really want to do or something you're doing to earn your family's love."

Barb: "I need to find out if I've made a big mistake."

Debbie: "You're unsure about what your own career needs are."

Barb: "Yeah. I'm not even sure how to make such an important decision myself."

Debbie: "You feel discouraged because you can't assert your own needs as indicated by your inability to make a decision."

Barb: "That's a pretty pathetic description of someone about to get her masters, but I guess it's accurate. I just kept doing what I thought my folks wanted and now here I am. . . ."

Debbie: "You're embarrassed by your inability to assert yourself and live your own life."

Barb: "Right. And I think it's about time I do something about that."

Debbie: "You're disappointed in yourself because you don't know how to make decisions and you want to learn to do so."

Barb: "Exactly! When I know how to make my own decisions then I'll know if I'm living my own life or just trying to prove something to my parents."

Debbie: "Now you're energized by the thought of taking control of your life. You want to learn to assert your own needs as indicated by knowing and acting upon the skills of decision making."

5
Initiating —
Facilitating
Helpee Acting

From the end of the first year, children draw from their repertoire of behaviors to produce the responses needed to achieve their goals. For example, children may laugh or cry to bring their parents to them. Children may move their hands in the direction of the unreachable food or objects. There may be a series of trial-and-error experiences. These experiences may confirm the children's responses through reaching the goals and experiencing satisfaction or they may modify the children's responses through not reaching the goals.

The children begin to act to get from where they are to where they want to be in their worlds. This is the third stage or phase of learning. It enables human beings to plan and work to influence their future.

Here are some questions you can ask as you begin to think about initiating:

How do you know when you have reached your goal?

How do you know when you are moving toward your goal?

How do you know when someone is assisting you in achieving your goal?

Case Study #7—Unskilled Initiating

Carol Snelling is an attractive 31-year-old woman. She has been married for twelve years and has two girls aged twelve and ten. Carol has come to a crisis intervention center with her two children, carrying a large suitcase. She has several bruises on her arms and one on her face, accompanied by a recent gash over her left eye. One of her daughters has recently had a bloody nose and one of her eyes is bruised. Carol originally came to the center because she and her children left home due to her husband's physical and emotional abuse. She was placed in a Battered Women's Shelter and returned to the center the next day to talk more extensively with a counselor.

Her counselor, Meg Mitchell, has been doing family counseling for several years. The following is an excerpt from their first session. The children are not present.

Carol: "It got so bad that I had to take the kids and leave. At first Steve just shouted. Then he started hitting me. Then he hit the kids. Also, it was happening more and more often. . . ." (crying) "I don't know what it is I do that sets him off. I've tried, but I always do something wrong."

Meg: "You're feeling guilty because Steve told you that you were why he was upset."

Carol: "That's right! He would yell at me or the kids about something and then he'd work himself into a frenzy. I'd get so scared. I'm worried right now because of what he might do if he finds me.''

Meg: "You're feeling scared because he still might hurt you or the children."

Carol: "Maybe I shouldn't have left. He's going to be so upset. . . .''

Meg: "You're feeling scared of what he might do and guilty because you left him."

Carol: "I know it sounds confusing, but I can't help it. I still love him! I just don't know how to keep him happy."

Meg: "You feel guilty because you love Steve but can't please him. You don't know what it is that you're doing wrong."

Carol: "Yes. But at the same time he shouldn't be beating me or the kids. That's wrong, too!''

Meg: "You're furious with Steve for his violence."

Carol: "I don't know who's more to blame. I know I'm not the best wife in the world. He's not the greatest husband. The kids can be a little much sometimes too."

Meg: "You feel overwhelmed because you don't know who exactly is responsible for what. All you know is that everyone has a part of the responsibility."

Carol: "That's right. Each of us has been doing something wrong."

Meg: "You feel miserable because you know that the family members have been hurting each other but you can't figure out how to change things."

Carol: "It's just beyond me. The whole thing becomes so confusing."

Meg: "You feel disappointed because you can't figure out how to get the family members to relate to one another the way they should."

Carol: "That's right."

Meg: "Carol, what you want, then, is to have you, Steve and the children build the kind of family relationships that will let everyone grow."

Carol: "Exactly what I want. But how do I do that?"

Meg: "You're saying that you don't know how to do that."

Carol: "Everything is such a mess that I don't know where to begin."

Meg: "Well, there isn't much we can do unless Steve and the kids get involved in therapy."

Carol: "Steve would never see a counselor.... He'd refuse. He thinks all shrinks are crazy. Oh, excuse me."

Meg: "That's all right, but without Steve we won't be able to accomplish anything. You're going to have to figure out a way to get him here."

Carol: "I don't think there's anything I can do to make him come. I don't know...."

Meg: "You have to try."

Carol: "All right, but what if he refuses?"

Meg: "Let's wait and see if you can get him here. O.K.?"

Carol: "Well, O.K."

Initiating is the culminating phase of helping. Initiating emphasizes facilitating the helpees' efforts to act to achieve their goals. In other words, the helpees act to change or gain in their functioning. This action is based upon their personalized understanding of their goals. It is facilitated by the helper's initiative.

Initiating involves defining goals, developing programs, designing schedules and reinforcements and individualizing steps. Defining the goals emphasizes the operations comprising the goals. Developing the programs emphasizes the steps needed to achieve the goals. Designing schedules emphasizes attaching time to steps while designing reinforcements emphasizes attaching reinforcements to steps. Individualizing emphasizes insuring that the steps are related to the helpees' frames of reference.

INITIATING FACILITATES HELPEE ACTING

While initiating is largely a series of mechanical activities based upon a personalized goal, the helper continues to function differentially according to the helpees' needs. The helper continues to emphasize empathic responsiveness. Having been additive in personalizing the understanding of the goal, the helper now drops back to interchangeable levels of responding. In so doing, the helper emphasizes individualizing the steps to the goals. In practice, this means that the helper is always checking back with the helpees in developing and implementing the programs.

In addition, the helper communicates conditional regard for the helpees. The helper has a clear picture of the helpees' assets and deficits and reinforces them conditionally in order to help them to develop and implement their programs effectively. All of this is communicated in a highly-genuine manner. Because both helper and helpees know one another well, they may now relate freely and openly as themselves. Finally, there is an increasing emphasis upon specificity or concreteness in developing and implementing the programs.

THE CORE CONDITIONS OF ACTING

PHASE III OF HELPING

HELPER DIMENSIONS	SKILLS LEVEL EMPHASIS
Empathy	Responding Inter-changeably
Respect	Communicating Conditional Regard
Genuineness	Being Fully Genuine
Concreteness	Being Fully Specific
	↓
HELPEE PROCESS	ACTING

PHASE III CORE HELPING SKILLS

Defining Goals

The most critical task in initiating is defining the goals. If we can define the goals in terms of the operations comprising the goals, then our direction is clear. We can answer the basic question of direction: "How will we know when we have reached our goal?"

In defining the goals, we will use our basic interrogatives in a creative way. We will define the operations of the goal in terms of the same 5WH interrogatives that we explored earlier: who, what, why, when, where, how. Now we will describe these interrogatives in terms of the operations of the goals: components, functions, processes, conditions, standards. These operations will establish all of the ingredients that we need to achieve our goals.

PERSONALIZING GOALS ➡ DEFINING GOALS

The first ingredient of our goals is the components. The components describe who and what are involved in the goal. Components are the nouns or labels that we attach to people or things.

Thus, for example, any of our helpees' problems in living may involve other people as the critical components. In learning problems, the components may involve ingredients such as the learning material or content as well as teachers or students. In working problems, the components tend to emphasize working tasks as well as superiors, subordinates and co-workers.

In defining the components, it is important to include all of the people or things involved. Sometimes third parties or indirect experiences or tasks may impinge upon the helpees' achievement of the goals.

THINK STEPS

WHAT is involved?

WHO is involved?

DEFINING COMPONENTS

The second ingredient in defining our goals is the functions. The functions describe what the people or things do. Functions are verbs that describe activities.

Thus, for example, our helpees' problems in living may involve performing interpersonal skills such as relating to loved ones in friendships or parent-child relationships. In learning, the functions may emphasize certain learning activities like receiving, acquiring, applying or transferring the learning. In working, the functions may emphasize certain working activities like expanding, narrowing, planning and implementing the performance of tasks.

In defining the functions, it is important to include all of the activities involved. That way no critical activity may be omitted in our attempts to achieve our goals.

THINK STEPS

WHAT is to be done?

WHO is doing it?

DEFINING FUNCTIONS

The third ingredient in defining our goals is the processes. The processes describe the reasons and the methods by which the components will accomplish the functions. Processes are adverbial phrases that modify the functions or activities.

Thus, for example, our helpees may learn to relate effectively by learning to respond accurately with interpersonal skills. In the learning area, the helpees may need to "learn-how-to-learn" in order to function effectively. In the working area, the helpees may need to learn problem-solving or decision-making skills in order to work productively. Again, it is important to be inclusive in defining these processes in order to avoid missing critical goal operations.

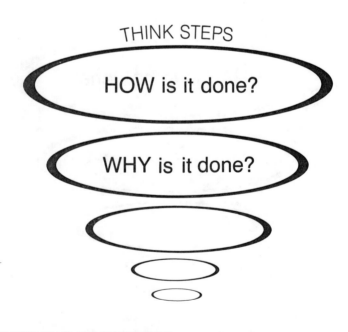

THINK STEPS

HOW is it done?

WHY is it done?

DEFINING PROCESSES

The fourth ingredient in defining our goals is the conditions. The conditions describe where and when the functions will occur. Conditions are also adverbial phrases that describe the functions.

For example, our helpees' interpersonal functioning could take place at home at mealtimes with parents or on evening dates with a girlfriend or boyfriend. Similarly, the helpees' learning could take place in the classroom at school during school hours and working could take place at the individual performance stations during working hours. Again, it is important to be specific about the conditions under which the functions will be performed so as to insure the completeness of the performance.

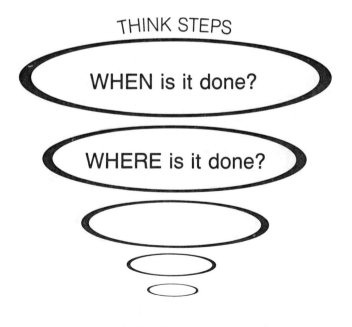

THINK STEPS

WHEN is it done?

WHERE is it done?

DEFINING CONDITIONS

The fifth and final ingredient in defining goals is the standards. The standards describe how well the functions are to be performed. The standards are also adverbial phrases describing the functions.

For example, our helpees' interpersonal functioning may require an extended base of communication of at least six interchangeable responses. Our helpees' learning skills may require an ability to explore, understand and act on each skill to be learned. Our helpees' working skills may require an ability to programmatically resolve a problem or make a decision.

Again, it is important to be very specific about the criteria of effectiveness. Otherwise, our helpees will not know when they have achieved their goals.

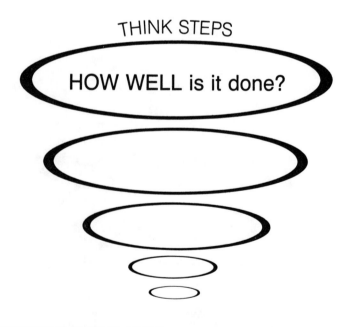

THINK STEPS

HOW WELL is it done?

DEFINING STANDARDS

The answers to these questions will define the operations of the goals we wish to achieve. The operations establish all of the ingredients that we need to know and do to achieve our helpees' goals. Above all, they define the standards of excellence in achieving our helpees' goals.

For example, we may summarize our definition of our helpee's goals for resolving an interpersonal problem with his parents as follows:

Components — Parents and helpee

Functions — To relate effectively

Processes — By responding accurately

Conditions — At home during mealtimes

Standards — By establishing an interchangeable base of communication (at least six responses)

Given this operational description, the helpee has a clear image of the goal. It remains for him to develop and implement a program to achieve the goal.

OPERATIONALIZING THE GOAL

We must now communicate our definition of the goal to the helpees in these operational terms. We do this by emphasizing the observable and measurable terms. These terms emphasize the standards of performance. Usually this means describing the goal in terms of the number of times or the amount of time the helpees will spend doing some behavior. In personalizing the goal, we use the personalizing format:

"You feel _____ because you cannot _____
and you want to _____ as
indicated by _____.
  (operational definition of goal)

In other words, we are answering the question, "How will I be able to tell when I have reached the goal?" We will want to practice defining the goal in our daily interactions and with recorded material such as the case studies.

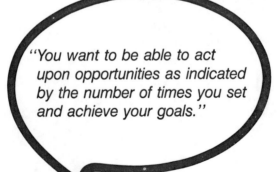

COMMUNICATING THE OPERATIONAL GOAL

Developing Programs

Defining goals is clearly not enough to achieve them. To achieve the goals, we need to develop programs. Programs are simply step-by-step procedures for achieving the goals. Given the definition of the goals, the programs are derived from the operations. Every step in the program should lead to accomplishing the operations involved in the goal.

Most programs are sequenced by contingency, i.e., each step is dependent upon the performance of the previous step. That is, we determine what steps we must perform as preconditions for the next step and, finally, the operations of the goal. In this context, an action program consists of an operational goal, a basic first step and the intermediary steps to the goal. The goal is where the helpees want or need to be. The first step is the most basic step beginning with where the helpees are. The intermediary steps are the steps that lead directly to the achievement of the goal: they lead from where the helpees are to where they want to be.

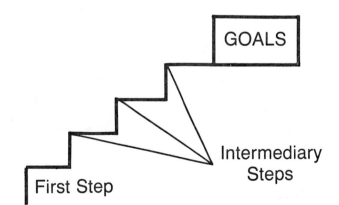

DEFINING GOALS ➡ DEVELOPING PROGRAMS

The first step is the most basic step that the helpee must take. It should be the most fundamental building block in the program. That way we can build the other steps upon it. For example, if the goal is running a mile in eight minutes, the first step might be walking around the block. For some people the first step to running a mile may literally and physically be taking a first step.

For our helpee the first step in relating to his parents might be attending to them. Indeed, the first step in learning or working may be attending to the task at hand. In communicating the first step, we use a simple straight-forward format.

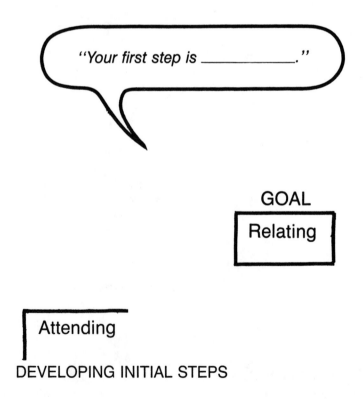

GOAL

Relating

Attending

DEVELOPING INITIAL STEPS

Intermediary steps bridge the gap between the first step and the goal. Our first intermediary step should be approximately halfway between the first step and the goal. For example, if the goal is running a mile in eight minutes, the first intermediary step might be running one-half mile or running a mile in 12 minutes.

For our helpee the first intermediary step in relating to his parents might be listening to them. Similarly, the first intermediary step in learning might be understanding the learning goal while the first intermediary step in working might be developing the task requirements. In communicating the first intermediary step, we use a direct, simple format.

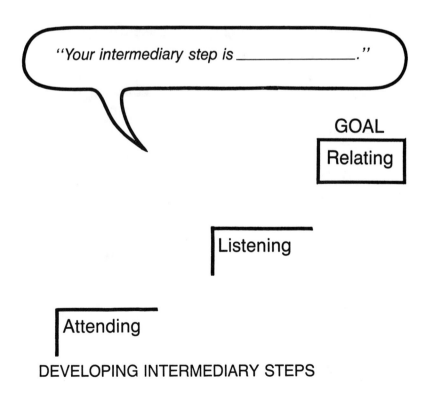

"Your intermediary step is _____."

GOAL

Relating

Listening

Attending

DEVELOPING INTERMEDIARY STEPS

We continue to fill out our program by developing sub-steps. We develop sub-steps by treating each step in the program as a sub-goal and developing the initial and intermediary steps to achieving that sub-goal. We continue to do this until we have all the steps needed to achieve our goal. If we leave out a step, our helpees will fail to achieve their goals. If we are planning to run a mile, we must develop distance and time substeps, moving, for example, from 1/4 to 1/2 to 3/4 to 1 mile and from 12 to 10 to 9 to 8 minutes.

With our helpee, the sub-steps to the relating goal might emphasize observing and responding skills. In turn, these skills can be treated as sub-goals and sub-steps can be developed to achieve the sub-goals just as we have in this book. We might develop similar exploring and acting sub-steps for a learning program and sub-steps of expanding options and selecting preferred courses for a working program. In communicating the sub-steps, we use a simple format.

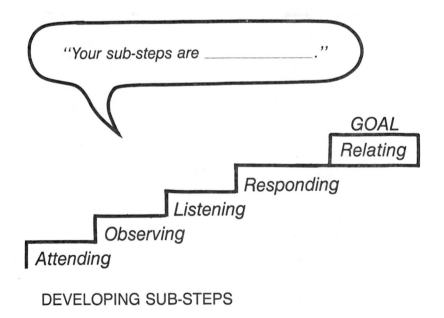

DEVELOPING SUB-STEPS

Developing Schedules

The process of initiating continues as we develop time schedules for step and goal achievement. Schedules serve to focus our programs. They close the gaps that might have been left by open-ended timelines.

The major emphasis in scheduling is on developing starting and finishing times. They tell both helper and helpees when things are to be done. Starting and finishing times may also be set for individual steps as well as for the overall program. No program is complete without a starting and finishing time.

DEVELOPING PROGRAMS ➤ DEVELOPING SCHEDULES

The first step in developing schedules is setting specific completion times or dates. For example, we might set a completion time of six months for achieving our goal of running a mile in eight minutes.

In our illustration, our helpee may aim to complete the relating program by the end of month five. Again, we may set similar completion times for any living, learning and working steps or goals. In communicating completion times, we may use a simple format.

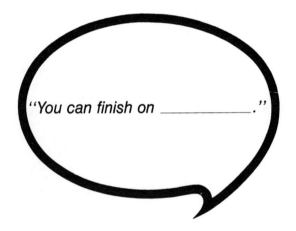

SETTING COMPLETION TIMES

The second step in developing schedules is setting specific starting times or dates. For example, we might start walking immediately to achieve our goal of running a mile in eight minutes.

With our helpee, we may set a starting time for the interpersonal skills program. We may set similar starting times for all living, learning and working steps and goals. In communicating starting times, we may use a simple and direct format.

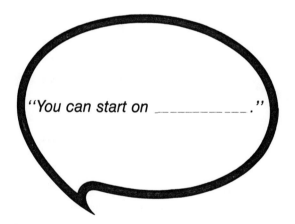

SETTING STARTING TIMES

In a similar manner, we can set starting and completion times for each interim step. The main purpose of setting schedules is to monitor the timelines of the helpees' performance of the steps of the program. For example, our helpee might decide that he would spend the next month learning and practicing how to pay attention. The first week he could concentrate upon preparing himself for attending; the second week upon attending by squaring; the third week upon attending by leaning; and the fourth week upon attending by making eye contact. A detailed schedule allows both helpee and helper to monitor the performance of steps.

"You can start _____ and finish in _____."

MONITORING TIMELINES

Developing Reinforcements

The next step in initiating involves developing reinforcements that will encourage the helpees to take the needed steps. Reinforcements are simply things that matter to us. They are most effective when they are applied immediately following our step performance.

The consequences of carrying out the steps to achieve their goals and overcome their deficits are often too distant for the helpees. More immediate reinforcements must be introduced.

Clearly, these reinforcements must come from the helpees' frames of reference. What we think matters for the helpees must really matter to them. Many helping programs have failed because of their inability to attach appropriate reinforcements. We all know the story of people who fuss to get attention because any attention—even negative—is more reinforcing than the reinforcements of their programs. In this context, we continue to emphasize our responsiveness: empathy is the source of all knowledge about powerful reinforcements for the helpees. Sometimes, it may be appropriate for helpees to work with support persons or groups to monitor their performance and administer the reinforcements.

DEVELOPING
SCHEDULES DEVELOPING
REINFORCEMENTS

Positive reinforcers or rewards are our most potent reinforcements. People tend to work hard for things that really matter to them. This means the helper must work diligently to develop the positive reinforcers from the helpees' frames of reference. In turn, the helpees must work diligently to receive the reinforcers.

Our helpee, for example, might decide simply that he would go out with his friends on Friday and Saturday nights as he completed each step. We can develop similar reinforcements for any and all living, learning and working programs. The reinforcements will vary as widely as the tastes of human nature itself.

"As you complete each step, you can _____."

REINFORCING POSITIVELY

To the degree we can, we want to avoid employing negative reinforcers. We use the term in a restricted sense to mean punishments. In this context, the application of negative reinforcers stimulates other reaction, such as aversive reactions to the person who administers the punishment. To avoid dealing with these reactions, initially we should attempt to define the negative reinforcers as the absence of rewards.

In our helpee's case, he defined his own negative reinforcers as forcing himself to stay home and work on the uncompleted step during the weekend evening hours. Again, similar negative reinforcers may be designed and applied in other living, learning and working programs. Like rewards, negative reinforcers vary widely and, to use them effectively, we must be finely tuned to the people involved.

REINFORCING NEGATIVELY

If it is not clear whether a step was performed in a satis-
factory manner, then we must observe the performer vigilantly. We do so to determine whether the person is
moving toward or away from the goal. Ultimately, all
behavior is either goal-directed or non-goal-directed.

Relatedly, we position ourselves as helpers to positively
reinforce the positive, goal-directed behavior of our
helpees and to negatively reinforce the negative, goal-less
behavior. It is as if we are aligning ourselves with what is
healthy in the individuals and in opposition to what is
unhealthy. We communicate our respect for them as people but not for their unhealthy behavior. We may use
ourselves most potently in being vigilantly conditional by
spelling out the implications of the helpees' behavior for
our own behavior.

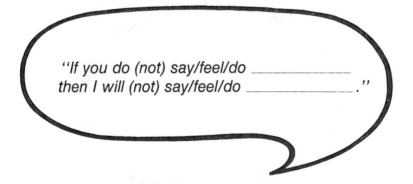

OBSERVING VIGILANTLY

Individualizing Steps

Most programs are comprised of steps that are sequenced by contingency, where each step is dependent upon the performance of the previous step. Some helpees cannot perform the steps readily as they are designed. They require programs individualized to their own particular learning or processing styles. The modes of individualizing include sequencing the steps from simple-to-complex, concrete-to-abstract and immediate-to-remote. Often these steps vary with those sequenced by contingency as well as with each other.

Actually, every step of initiating should be individualized by checking back with the helpees. We check back with the helpees by making interchangeable responses that insure that we are in tune with the helpees' frames of reference. Even when we individualize the sequencing of steps, we must stay finely tuned because this is a very subtle human process.

DEVELOPING   ➤   INDIVIDUALIZING
REINFORCEMENTS   STEPS

The most basic of the alternative sequencing modalities is the simple-to-complex method. Here some helpees may work most productively with those steps that are most simple. Often these steps will vary from those sequenced by contingency.

In developing simple steps, we often say that the first step should be so simple as to be absurd. That way we can be sure that the helpees can achieve it. For example, with our helpee we may begin our attending skills program with facing the other person, a most-simple step that can be performed readily. It is a still-more-simple step than the squaring step that would be dictated by contingency. We may spend some time reflecting upon the individual differences we might design into programs sequenced by contingency or from simple-to-complex.

"You can do the most simple step first."

SEQUENCING SIMPLE-TO-COMPLEX STEPS

Another alternative sequencing modality is the concrete-to-abstract mode. Here some helpees may work most productively with those tasks that are most concrete. In this context, some helpees may consider beginning an interpersonal skills program with concrete steps such as developing programs which would come much later in a contingency-sequenced program. Let us see how many more instances of differences in sequencing we may develop in a variety of living, learning and working programs. These differences are what allow us to individualize the programs.

"You can do the most concrete step first."

SEQUENCING CONCRETE-TO-ABSTRACT STEPS

The final and in some ways most interesting mode of individualizing is the immediate-to-remote method. Here some helpees prefer steps that begin with their immediate experiences. For example, in an interpersonal skills program, some helpees may prefer to begin by learning to respond to a real-life problem even though this is a much later step in a contingency-sequenced program. Again, let us expand our thinking about the alternate sequencing modalities. It is critical that we employ the individualizing modalities by staying tuned with our individualizing, interchangeable responses.

"You can do the most immediate step first."

SEQUENCING IMMEDIATE-TO-REMOTE STEPS

Summary

One way of structuring initiating is to test the comprehensiveness of our initiative responses to the helpees' experience. Let us simply attend, respond and personalize in our next encounter. Then let us attempt to rate the effectiveness of our initiative response to the helpees' experiences as follows:

High initiative — Implementing steps

Moderate initiative — Defining goals

Low initiative — Personalizing goals

As can be seen, the low levels of initiative are consistent with the high levels of personalizing (goal). The moderate levels of initiative involve defining goals while the high levels involve implementing steps.

We can now complete our cumulative scale for helping. If the helper is attending, responding, personalizing and initiating the steps to achieve the operational goal, then the helper is operating at a fully-initiative level (level 5.0). If the helper is initiating only to define the goal, then the helper can be rated at an initiative level (level 4.5).

LEVELS OF HELPING

5.0	Initiating steps
4.5	Defining goals
4.0	Personalizing goals
3.5	Personalizing meaning
3.0	Responding to meaning
2.5	Responding to feeling
2.0	Responding to content
1.5	Attending personally
1.0	Nonattending

LEVELS OF HELPING: ATTENDING, RESPONDING, PERSONALIZING AND INITIATING

Developing initiative is the culminating act in the helping process. Given personalized goals, initiating enables us to define the goals and develop the programs to achieve the goals. Resolving the helpees' problems and achieving their goals is what helping is all about.

Again, while the development of initiative is a mechanical process, it must also be an individualized process. We must constantly check back with the helpees' frames of reference by making accurate responses to their experiences. At the highest levels of helping, responding and initiating are integrally related. There is no real understanding without action. There is no real action without understanding.

PHASES OF HELPING

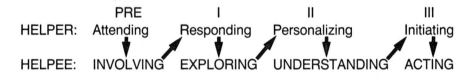

INVOLVING, EXPLORING, UNDERSTANDING AND ACTING

You now know about all of the basic helping skills: attending, responding, personalizing and initiating. You will need to work in a most intense and disciplined manner to learn to acquire and apply these skills. Practice until you can process these responses fluidly and effectively as part of your own helping personality as in the following case study.

Case Study #8—Skilled Initiating

In a group of substance abusers are three men and one woman. Zeke is a 19-year-old college dropout who referred himself to treatment after an overdose of alcohol and tranquilizers that almost killed him. Frank is a 25-year-old who is in treatment as a condition of his probation for grand larceny. His drug of choice was cocaine. Lu Anne, who is usually called Muffin, is a 17-year-old chronic runaway who was referred to treatment by her parents after her last run. She has been a multiple drug user. Mitch is a 22-year-old college student who was referred to treatment by a friend. He stated he was having problems with "pot" and alcohol.

Lois, the helper, is an attractive woman in her mid-thirties. She has been a substance abuse counselor for the last five years. She has never had a problem with drugs or alcohol herself.

The room is set up with chairs and a chart pad in a circle. The room is bright and cheery. There are no antidrug or alcohol posters on the walls. There are several very good, dramatic water color portraits of people expressing intense emotions.

(This is an excerpt from the third counseling session. It starts about ten minutes into the session.)

Lois: "Frank, you're looking irritated, with that scowl on your face."

Zeke: "Yeah, what's bothering you?"

Lois: "It sounds like some of the others have noticed it, too".

Frank: "It's not anything I really want to talk about."

Muffin: "Okay, it's hard to open up, but that's one of the reasons why we're here; because we don't really communicate."

Frank: "Listen you little _____, when I want your advice I'll ask for it!"

Lois: "You're really torn up by what's bothering you. You're so angry you're lashing out at anyone."

Frank: "Hey, Muffin, I'm sorry. . .I just. . .I don't know."

Muffin: "Listen, I've been called worse. It's okay."

Lois: "You feel frightened because you aren't sure what we might say or do if you tell us what's concerning you."

Frank: "It's not that I don't trust you. . .It's just personal."

Zeke: "It is really hard to start opening up to people you hardly know."

Lois: "Frank, you're struggling with something that's really overwhelming and you don't want to lose control."

Frank: (silence, looking at the floor, trembling noticeably) "Yeah."

Lois: (gets up from her chair, squats down in front of Frank, and takes his hands) "You're in so much pain that you can hardly stand it." (Frank bursts into tears and hugs Lois. Muffin and Zeke, who are sitting next to Frank, each put a hand on his shoulder. Mitch sits watching, looking uncomfortable. After about a minute Frank starts to calm down. Lois hands him a kleenex.)

Frank: "I'm sorry. I've never done anything like that before. . .it's just. . ." (he blows his nose) "it hurts so bad."

Muffin: "So tell us what has you so torn to pieces."

Frank: "I've been dating this girl for the last few weeks. I really like her. I thought we had something special going. Things were going fine, but then someone told her about my drug use and my record.

"Now, she doesn't want to see me again. She said that I had lied to her, that I didn't tell her the truth about myself. I wanted to tell her about what I've been through; I just didn't know how."

Zeke: "Wow."

Lois: "You're really devastated by your girl friend confronting you and leaving you."

Frank: "Yeah, it really hurts. But the tough part is that I really have a difficult time meeting people. She was just about the only person outside this room I could talk to who isn't into drugs."

Muffin: "Yeah, I know what you mean. I don't have anyone either. I tried a couple of times, but no one wanted to have anything to do with me."

Lois: "Frank, you feel really frightened because of how lonely the world is for you. And Muffin, you sound really angry because you've tried to reach out and have been rebuffed."

Muffin: "At least when I was into drugs, sex and rock and roll, I wasn't so lonely."

Lois: "You feel humiliated because you think straight kids won't have anything to do with you."

Muffin: "Yeah, they all think I'm a whore. They won't have anything to do with me. I mean, at least when I did drugs I could shut off all this stuff. At least then I had friends."

Lois: "You're frightened because you don't think you'll be able to relate to another person without drugs."

Muffin: "I've messed up my life so bad I can't believe that anyone could like me. I mean I've done some sick, sick things when I've been high. Who'd want me?"

Lois: "You're terrified because you don't believe you can find any other way to be wanted."

Muffin: (tears on her cheeks) "I guess I'm not as tough as I thought."

Mitch: "Muffin? . . ." (She looks up. He reaches over to her hesitantly.) "I don't really know how to say this, but I think you're being too tough on yourself." (Muffin makes a hesitant smile.)

Lois: "You seem to be having the same feeling of hurt and fear of being alone, Mitch."

Mitch: (hesitantly) "Yeah, well . . ."

Zeke: "Boy, I sure can relate to what she's saying. I mean, I look back on my life and am so . . . ashamed! I just can't believe I can be any different. Who'd want to know a sleaze ball like me, you know?"

Lois: "You feel disgusted and ashamed, too. You don't know how to start fresh with people." (turning back to Mitch) "But, Mitch, I was hearing more pain, more yearning in your voice, rather than shame or disgust."

Mitch: "Yeah, I've been so lonely and so scared of people. I guess that's why I drank and smoked dope. It helped me feel powerful and in control, you know."

Lois: "So you feel frightened because you don't know how to relate to people either."

Mitch: "That's right."

Lois: "Frank, you feel hurt because you don't know if you can find someone to relate with. Muffin, you're scared that you'll never be able to experience real intimacy with someone. Mitch, you're frightened because you're unsure how to start a relationship. And you, Zeke, are disappointed because you don't know if you can have a decent relationship." (multiple "Yeah" and "That's right.")

Muffin: "So what do we do?"

Lois: "Although your reasons are a little different, it seems each of you is saying that you're frightened and hurt because you cannot find a way to make new friends and each of you wants to start fresh, healthy relationships." (Lois looks at each person with an inquiring look. All nod their heads.) "Or put another way, each of you is looking for a way to relate to other people without having to use drugs."

Mitch: "That's it exactly!" (multiple "Yeses" and "That's it!")

Lois: "Although each of you might have slightly different reasons for developing friendships, we need to start with learning how to relate."

Frank: "We really have to start at the beginning."

Lois: "Exactly. Each of you has to learn to relate to another person as yourself rather than when you're high."

Zeke: "But how will we know if we're relating right or not?"

Lois: "You're looking for a way to tell if you're relating properly or not."

Muffin: "That's easy. For me, it's if the person wants to see me again."

Frank: "For me, it's if the person shares something special with me."

Zeke: "I guess for me it's if the person enjoys being with me."

Lois: "You haven't said anything, Mitch."

Mitch: "I don't know. I guess it's the same as with Muffin."

Lois: "Okay, Zeke, Frank, it seems that if someone is willing to see you again, more than likely that person enjoys your company and will be willing to be self-disclosing with you."

Zeke: "Yeah, I guess."

Frank: "Sure."

Lois: "So we can use the willingness of the other person to interact with you again as an indication of how well you're relating."

Muffin: "That'll be a real trick. I can't even get them to talk to me the first time!"

Lois: "It's hard for you to even get an initial conversation started. Well, the very first thing we need to learn is how to greet people and get them involved with us. We also want to be able to size them up to see if we want them as friends."

Mitch: "I never know what to say."

Lois: "So learning how to do that makes sense for you. The next thing might be how to get them to talk about themselves."

Zeke: "Hey, yeah, If they think you're really interested in them they're more likely to become a friend."

Lois: "That's right. You're beginning to sound pleased with this. And the next step is getting them to want to intensify the relationship."

Muffin: "Can we really do this?"

Lois: "You're pretty surprised that learning how to make new friends is possible."

Muffin: "Boy, I thought I'd never be able to fit in with anyone but the freaks."

Lois: "You're feeling relieved because now there seems to be some hope."

Muffin: "When can we get started?"

Lois: "You want to get going right now?" (Zeke and Frank simultaneously, "Yeah!") "Okay. First we'll learn how to decide on who we want as new friends. Then we'll learn how to get them to talk about themselves. And finally we'll learn how to intensify a relationship.''

Mitch: "You really can teach us that?''

Lois: "You're questioning if I can deliver what I've said. And yet you sound hopeful.''

Mitch: "Boy, I really want to learn.''

Lois: "And I want to teach you. We'll start right now. We'll probably need the next three sessions to teach you the skills.''

Zeke: "I'm really excited. Maybe I can change my life.''

Lois: "You're really feeling relieved because you think you have a chance now.''

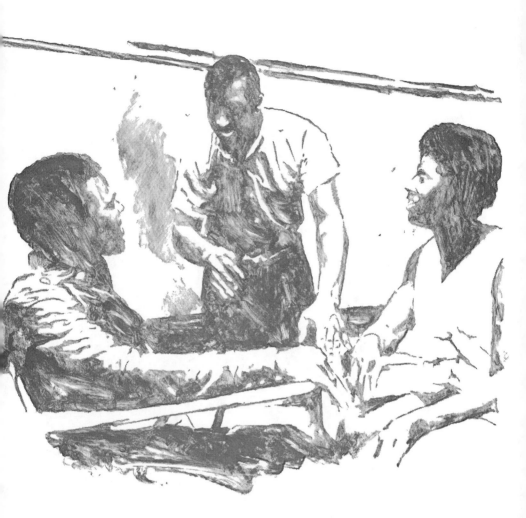

6
Helping —
Recycling Helpee
Processing

The first year of human development serves as a prototype for all human learning. Initially, the children explore and identify the nature of specific stimuli and responses. Transitionally, the children come to understand the interactive nature of stimuli and responses, anticipate the effect of one upon the other and develop goals to achieve these effects. Finally, the children act by drawing from their developing repertoire of responses to attempt to achieve their goals. The children's behavior is shaped by the feedback, achieved in the environment. This feedback recycles the stages or phases of learning as children explore more extensively, understand more accurately and act more effectively. This ascending, enlarging spiral of exploring, understanding and acting is the source of adults' improving repertoire of responses.

Here are some questions you can ask as you begin to think about recycling the helping process:

How do you know whether your action is effective?

How do you use the feedback you get?

How do you increase your effectiveness in life?

Case Study #9—Skilled Helping

HELPEE INVOLVING/ HELPER ATTENDING		TYPE OF RESPONSE
Floyd:	"Man, I don't see how this jive is gonna get us anywhere! We've tried working together, but I don't see how we can."	
Helper:	"It's pretty frustrating to try working these things through without anyone's help. If you're free the next hour, I'd like to get together with you in my office."	Informing
Tom:	"It's O.K. with me, I guess."	
Helper:	"What about you, Floyd? I'd like to spend a little time getting to know both of you better. Then I'll be able to be more helpful."	Encouraging
Floyd:	"What about a cup of coffee instead?"	
Helper:	"Coffee's fine. I can really learn as much right here as in my office."	Attending Contextually
Floyd:	"What do you want to learn about us?"	
Tom:	"Yeah, I mean, I know you've been checking us out for quite a while."	

Helper:	"So you've been using your observing skills, too. You've noticed that I've really been paying attention to you."	Attending Personally
Tom:	"Uh huh. What have you been—you know—learning from us?"	
Helper:	"Well, I see two young guys who care enough about each other to stay in there fighting with each other. One's maybe more worn out than he should be and the other one's kind of edgy."	Observing
Floyd:	"You've really been using your eyes to see us, huh?"	
Helper:	". . . And my ears to hear, too."	Listening

HELPEE EXPLORING/ HELPER RESPONDING		TYPE OF RESPONSE
Floyd:	"The thing that really hassles me is the way you all act like everything's cool and I'm just supposed to relax and keep smiling!"	
Helper:	"You're saying it really gets to you when whites seem to want you to lay back and accept things."	Responding to Content
Tom:	"Man, we're all in this thing together! What's so special about you?"	
Helper:	"You don't see why Floyd has to make a special case out of himself."	Responding to Content

Floyd: "You don't see it, huh Tom? Well maybe if you woke up black one morning a lot of things'd come clearer to you!"

Helper: "You feel really angry."

Responding to Feeling

Floyd: "Yeah, right! I mean, no white person can know what it's like to be black."

Helper: "You feel really furious when someone who isn't black tries to tell you how to act."

Responding to Meaning

Tom: "You got a lot of nerve to come on like that to me, man!"

Helper: "It makes you angry when Floyd doesn't seem to appreciate the way you act with him."

Responding to Meaning

Floyd: "Listen, you get treated like an individual. But me—either I get turned down flat, or else everyone wants to get alongside of my blackness without ever checking out who I really am on the inside."

Helper: "It burns you up that people never seem to get past your skin to what's underneath."

Responding to Meaning

Floyd: "Damn straight! I could be a genius or a flat-out fool and it still wouldn't matter as much as the fact that I'm black!"

Helper:	"It drives you wild because people just see how you look without ever caring what you do or how you feel."	Responding to Meaning
Tom:	"Listen, you're doing the same thing when you lump me in with every other white!"	
Helper:	"You feel angry and frustrated because Floyd doesn't see the ways you try to relate to him as an individual."	Responding to Meaning
Floyd:	"It's not the same thing, man. It's not like being black."	

HELPEE UNDERSTANDING/ HELPER PERSONALIZING		TYPE OF RESPONSE
Floyd:	"Dig it! They don't know who I am and they really aren't open to finding out."	
Helper:	"It really gets you down because you're not seen as a real person."	Personalizing Meaning
Tom:	"I'm trying—I really am, but for him I'm just another 'whitey.' "	
Helper:	"You're frustrated because you're just another white."	Personalizing Meaning
Floyd:	"Listen! It's a real drag—like having to run 10 miles just to warm up for a 100-yard dash. Like—well, take writing, for one. I tried to get on the board at the Lit. Magazine. But once they found out I wasn't into writing heavy race-type stuff, they weren't interested."	

Helper:	"It's infuriating because you can't find a way to get people to treat you like an individual in your own right."	**Personalizing Problems**
Tom:	"I feel the same way, man. If I could just convince you I really do see you as a person and not just a black."	
Helper:	"Tom, you get bummed out because you don't feel like a real person when Floyd sees you as just another white."	**Personalizing Problems**
Floyd:	"If I could just get through to people."	
Helper:	"You feel helpless because you can't get other people—especially Tom—to see you the way you really are."	**Personalizing Feelings**
Tom:	"In a way I'm in the same boat. Maybe I don't feel it as strongly as if I were black but it seems like the same thing to me."	
Helper:	"You feel like you're in the same boat—discouraged because you can't get the real you across to Floyd."	**Personalizing Feelings**
Floyd:	"I've got a lot to offer. I mean really, I'm into a lot of good things I'd like to share. Like—well, like my writing."	

Helper: "Floyd, you feel miserable
because you can't get other peo-
ple to see what you really have to   **Personalizing**
offer and you want to very badly."   **Goals**

Tom: "Listen, Floyd, there's nothing I'd
like more than for you and me to
get beyond this lame race stuff.
I'd like for you to trust me and
share with me."

Helper: "And Tom, you feel pretty low
because you can't get Floyd to
understand you and you really
want to get him to see beyond   **Personalizing**
your whiteness."   **Goals**

HELPEE ACTING/   **TYPE OF**
HELPER INITIATING   **RESPONSE**

Helper: "So Floyd, you want other people
to see you as an individual. And
Tom, you want Floyd to see you
as an individual. How could you
each tell if you were reaching   **Defining the**
those goals?"   **Goals**

Floyd: "A good indication for me would
be if I could get on the board of
the Literary Magazine without having to be the 'racial reporter.' "

Tom: "I'd just like to get rid of all my
behaviors that Floyd feels are
racist, so we can get beyond the
color of our skins."

Helper: "O.K. Those sound like pretty
realistic goals. Floyd, your first
step might be to make a list of
real contributions you feel you
could make to the magazine's

operation. And Tom, your first step might be to ask Floyd what the things are that you do which he feels are basically racist." **Initiating First Step**

Floyd: "Hmm! That sounds O.K."

Tom: "Hey, I'm ready if you are."

Helper: "Tom, your next step could be to work with Floyd to prioritize which particular behaviors you should try to eliminate first. And Floyd, yours could be to find out what specific things a person has to do to be elected to the board." **Initiating Intermediate Steps**

Tom: "I got you."

Floyd: "Yeah, you're making a whole lot of sense."

Helper: "When do you think you could be done with these beginning steps?" **Initiating Schedules**

Floyd: "I can be done in a day or two."

Tom: "If Floyd has time, I could work on it tonight and tomorrow night."

Helper: "O.K. You might also decide to reward yourselves for completing a step by doing something you really enjoy doing. If you fail to take the step, you don't get the reward." **Initiating Reinforcements**

Floyd: "That's O.K. with me."

Tom: "Wow, the way you lay it all out it seems so easy! I can handle that for sure!"

Helper: "You feel a lot more hopeful because you begin to see how you can actually get where you want to go." **Responding to Meaning**

Recycling is the ongoing processing that produces more and more effective acting. It does so by using the feedback from action to stimulate more extensive exploring, more accurate understanding and more effective acting. Developing more effective responses is the means by which people grow. Helping is the process that facilitates recycling.

There are some additional skills involved in implementing initiating. These skills facilitate the recycling of exploring, understanding and acting. These recycling skills help us to improve our actions. They include implementing steps, check steps and recycling steps. They also include applications in group processes and teaching as treatment. Together, these skills facilitate the recycling of exploring, understanding and acting.

RECYCLING FACILITATES   E — U — A

The recycling skills take place in the context of the core conditions of recycling. These conditions involve subtle but important changes in the core dimensions of empathy, respect, genuineness and concreteness.

Perhaps the most important of these changes is the change in empathy. Empathy shifts to a kind of immediacy in the helper and, increasingly with recycling, the helpee. Immediacy means understanding and interpreting in the moment what is going on between people. It means living fully in the moment through responding fully to the helpees' experiences and initiating fully from our own experience.

Relatedly, respect evolves to differential regard. Differential regard emphasizes reinforcing constructive behavior positively; reinforcing destructive behavior negatively; and vigilantly observing all helpee behavior in order to determine its direction.

As helpers become increasingly immediate in empathy and differential in respect, they become increasingly transparent in genuineness. This means simply that we can see through them because they are freely and fully engaged in processing in the moment.

Finally, concreteness becomes programmatic. Just as we developed initiative programmatically by defining the goals and programs, so will we facilitate programmatic consideration of all specific details needed to succeed in life. The great irony is that the more programmatic we become, the more free we become and vice versa.

THE CORE CONDITIONS OF RECYCLING

RECYCLING PHASES

HELPER DIMENSIONS	SKILLS LEVEL EMPHASIS
Empathy	Responding with Immediacy
Respect	Communicating Differential Regard
Genuineness	Being Transparent
Concreteness	Being Programmatic

HELPEE PROCESS

$$\text{E} \rightarrow \text{U} \rightarrow \text{A}$$

RECYCLING CORE HELPING SKILLS

Implementing Steps

Now that we are ready to implement the programs we find that there still are steps necessary before our final implementation. We may call these our implementation steps although they are the final steps of preparation before implementation.

The critical implementation steps emphasize reviewing, rehearsing and revising the steps of the program. Reviewing insures the inclusiveness of our steps. Rehearsing helps us find the problems involved in implementing the steps. Revising emphasizes the final changes in the implementation program. Together, these steps prepare us for the final implementation step: recycling all previous steps. These detailed steps are only necessary if we wish to succeed.

INDIVIDUALIZING STEPS➡IMPLEMENTING STEPS

The first implementation step emphasizes reviewing all the steps of the program. In so doing, we must review our definitions of goals, steps of programs, times of schedules, consequences of reinforcements and modalities of individualizing. In our running program, we must check all distances and time steps. In implementing the interpersonal relating program, our helpee must begin by reviewing all steps of attending personally, observing, listening and responding. Again, reviewing gives us a chance to make sure that we have included all necessary steps in the program.

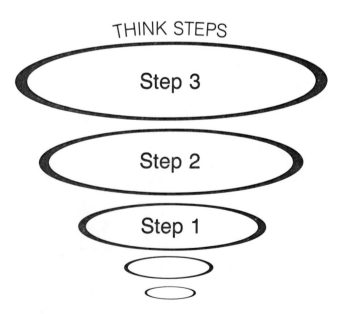

THINK STEPS

Step 3

Step 2

Step 1

REVIEWING STEPS

The second implementation step emphasizes rehearsing all the steps of the program. In so doing, we get a chance to pilot our final performance. Rehearsing gives us the opportunity to find the problems involved in the final implementation of the steps. For example, in our running program, we can try ourselves out in real-life running situations. In implementing the interpersonal attending program, our helpee may rehearse all of the attending and responding steps of his relating program. Again, rehearsal is only necessary if there are implications attached to our failure—i.e., if we do care about being successful.

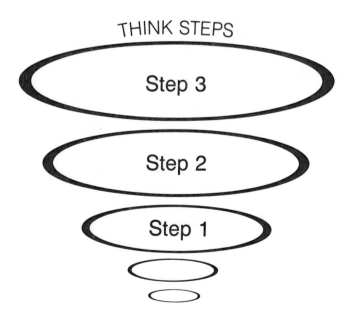

THINK STEPS

Step 3

Step 2

Step 1

REHEARSING STEPS

The third implementation step emphasizes revising all necessary steps of the program. The purpose of reviewing and rehearsing is revising. In revising, we recycle all of the necessary revisions in the steps of the program. We will revise the program again, when we get the feedback from our action step. In our running program, we may revise our time and distance estimates upward and downward. In implementing the interpersonal attending program, our helpee may revise some of the steps or sub-steps in order to increase the effectiveness of his action. For example, he may make successive approximations of certain steps in attending, like eye contact, in order to minimize calling attention to his changed behavior. Revising insures our probability of succeeding.

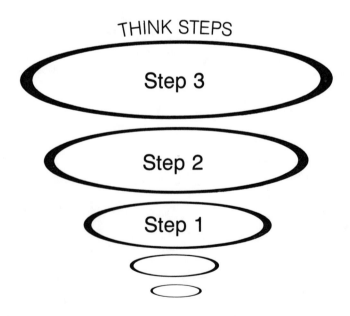

THINK STEPS

Step 3

Step 2

Step 1

REVISING STEPS

Initiating Check Steps

Just when we think we are ready to act, we find that we need to develop more steps in our programs. Again, we only need to do this if succeeding matters to us. If our goals are unimportant to us, then we can chance "giant" steps and risk failure. If our goals are important to us, then we must develop detailed programs and insure success.

One of the ways of building in success is to develop check steps. Check steps emphasize the things we need to think about before, during and after the performance of each program step. They emphasize the resources we need to be successful and the ways we need to monitor and assess our effectiveness in performing the steps.

IMPLEMENTING STEPS ➡ CHECK STEPS

The before check steps emphasize the things we need to do before we perform each step. They ask and answer the question: What resources will I need to perform the step successfully? These resources include physical, emotional and intellectual resources. For example, in planning to run a mile, physically we need a measured distance and stopwatch as well as some appropriate kind of running shoes and clothes. Emotionally we need motivation for achieving our goal and intellectually we need a step-by-step program. In implementing the inter-personal attending program, our helpee may need an appropriate physical setting, furniture, occasion and peo-ple such as that provided by mealtime in his home. In addition, he needs an emotional commitment and an intellectual program to achieve his goal. Without the resources, we are not able to perform the steps effec-tively. The before check steps give us an opportunity to check out our resources before performing the steps.

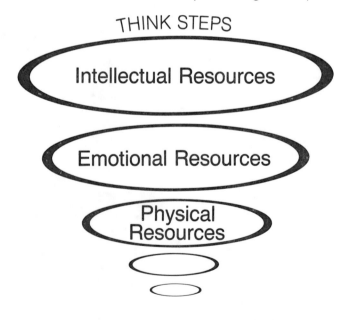

THINK STEPS

Intellectual Resources

Emotional Resources

Physical Resources

BEFORE CHECK STEPS

During check steps emphasize the things we need to do during the performance of each step. They ask and answer the question: Am I performing the step correctly? Again, correctness involves physical, emotional and intellectual dimensions. Physically, in running, we may check our times and distances. Emotionally, we may check out our level of motivation. Intellectually, we may check whether we are running with proper form or appropriate breathing. In implementing the interpersonal attending program, our helpee may check physically whether he is squared with others, leaning forward at a 10° angle, sitting forward at a 20° angle or making eye contact. Emotionally, he may check whether he is being fully attentive to others. Intellectually, he may check whether he is focused on the content and feeling of the others' expressions. The during check steps give us an opportunity to check ourselves out during the performance of the steps.

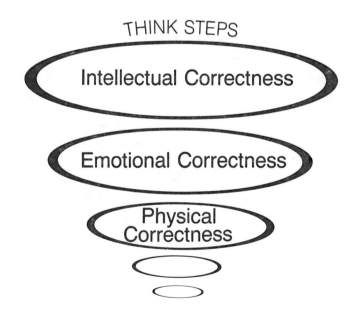

THINK STEPS

Intellectual Correctness

Emotional Correctness

Physical Correctness

DURING CHECK STEPS

After check steps emphasize the things we need to do after the performance of each step. They ask and answer the question: Did I perform the step effectively? Effectiveness has several levels of consideration. These include the antecedent or causative behaviors. They also include the consequences or the effects of the behaviors. Finally, they include the benefits that are derived from the effects. For example, in implementing the running program, we may check the antecedent behaviors, i.e., whether we ran the intended distance within the targeted time; we may check whether the antecedent behaviors affected the fitness consequences; and we may check whether the consequences did indeed lead to the desired benefits of leading full lives. In implementing the interpersonal attending program, our helpee may check whether he did indeed attend effectively to the others. He may also check whether the attentiveness facilitated his parents' involvement in a conversational process with him. Finally, he may check whether the conversational consequences led to the desired benefits of an improved relationship.

THINK STEPS

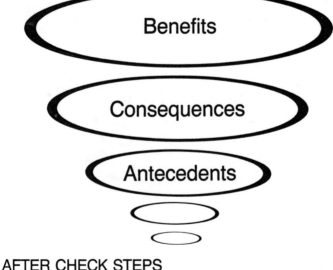

AFTER CHECK STEPS

Recycling Steps

After you have learned everything about helping and processing, then you must learn about the value of recycling. Our future growth and development lies in recycling our helping and processing skills. We may use these helping skills with ourselves as well as with others. They will serve to facilitate our own processing.

Clearly, the core of the recycling skills are the processing skills we have already learned: exploring, understanding and acting. With the feedback that we receive from the environment for our previous action, we recycle the helping process: responding to facilitate exploring more extensively; personalizing to facilitate understanding more accurately; and initiating to facilitate acting more effectively.

CHECK STEPS ➡ RECYCLING STEPS

Recycling exploring steps implies attempting to respond to achieve more extensive exploration of the helpees experiences. For example, in implementing the running program, we may receive some time or distance feedback that causes us to re-explore our fitness programs. The feedback may cause us to explore other dimensions of running or other means of becoming fit. In the interpersonal skills attending program, our helpee may explore other ways of attending to others or he may move on to applying his observing and listening skills. In recycling exploring, we are simply using the feedback to stimulate more extensive exploring about going back or moving on or modifying steps in our original program.

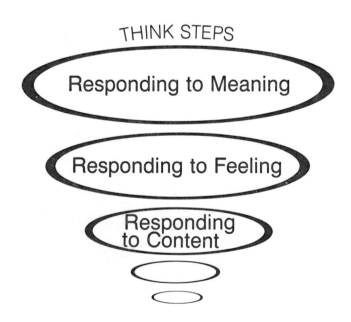

THINK STEPS

Responding to Meaning

Responding to Feeling

Responding to Content

EXPLORING STEPS

Similarly, recycling understanding steps implies attempting to achieve a more accurate understanding of our goals by further personalizing the helpees' experiences. For example, in the running program, the recycling of exploring may cause us to consider new time and distance or fitness goals. In the interpersonal attending program, our helpee may set new goals in attending or move on to new goals in other skill areas. In recycling understanding, we are simply using the new base of exploring to develop new goals for acting.

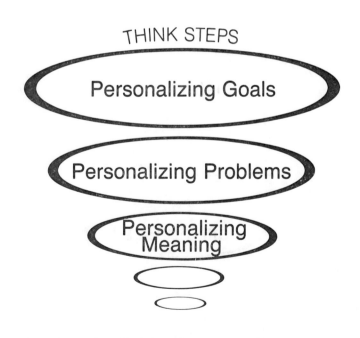

THINK STEPS

Personalizing Goals

Personalizing Problems

Personalizing Meaning

UNDERSTANDING STEPS

Finally, recycling acting steps implies initiating more effective action programs to achieve the new goals. For example, in the running program, the new goals may cause us to develop new programs to achieve the goals. In the interpersonal attending program, our helpee may develop new steps in attending or move on to developing or implementing new steps to achieve the new goals. In recycling acting, we are simply using our understanding of new goals to develop new action programs to achieve those goals. We then go on to recycle again the feedback from our acting. The cycle of processing is the cycle of learning in life.

THINK STEPS

Initiating Steps

Developing Programs

Defining Goals

ACTING STEPS

Applying Helping Skills to Group Processes

We can do anything with groups that we can do with individuals. That is not to say there is no place for individual helping. Nor is it to say that we cannot help individuals simultaneously while working with them in groups. It is to say that for most human problems, group processes are the most efficient and effective modes of treatment. A helper can see multiple helpees at once. A helper can affect helpee outcomes as good or better than through individual helping. The value of shared experiences is inestimable for both individual and group problems. Group processes are the preferred modes of helping.

It is helpful to think of the groups as individuals. We are merely attending to facets of the individual. In this context, the groups may be heterogeneous with a mix of people and problems or homogeneous with similar people and problems. Heterogeneity offers a more extensive experiential base preparing helpees for a variety of life situations. Homogeneity offers a more intense focus upon specific life problems.

The ingredients of group processes are similar to those of individual helping: involving group members; exploring group and individual experiences; understanding group and individual goals; acting upon group and individual programs; and recycling in groups.

GROUP PROCESSES —
A PREFERRED MODE OF HELPING

In attending to helpees or prospective helpees in order to involve them in the group processes, we use the same generic helping skills as we did in individual helping: preparing the helpees, the context and ourselves for helping; attending personally; observing; and listening. The only real difference between individual and group helping is that we attend to multiple people.

This means that the helpers must position themselves and the helpees to attend to all other helpees in the group. Usually, a circle is most facilitative of mutual attending. The helpers must simultaneously observe both the presenting helpees and the other members as well, viewing the same physical, emotional and intellectual dimensions of helpee functioning. Similarly, the helpers must listen with one ear to the individual and another to the group to hear the helpees and the content expressed. Again, for the helpers, the group is an individual, to be attended and involved in helping as if one person.

PHASES OF HELPING

	PRE
HELPER:	Attending
	↓
HELPEE:	INVOLVING
	Group Members

INVOLVING GROUP MEMBERS

Again, in responding, the helpers must respond to
unique individual as well as common group experiences.
Treating the groups as an individual, the helpers respond
to the common themes of the group as they would to
individual expressions of an individual. The helpers
respond to the multiple contents, feelings and meanings
of the group as well as individuals within the group. In so
doing, they use the format for feeling and meaning as
follows: "You feel _____ because _____ while
he/she feels _____ because _____."

PHASES OF HELPING

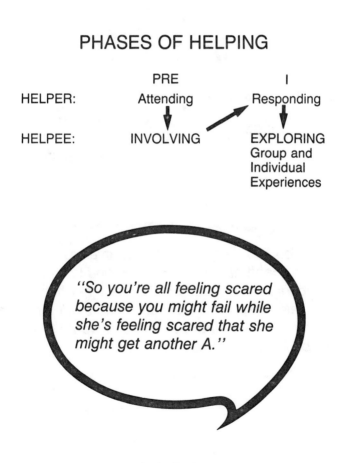

EXPLORING GROUP EXPERIENCES

Similarly, in personalizing, the helpers concentrate upon individual as well as group themes. The helpers summarize the dominant group themes and personalize the meaning, problems, goals and attendant feelings. At the same time, they personalize the unique experiences of the various individuals involved. In so doing they use the format for personalizing group and individual problems and goals: "You feel _____ because you cannot _____ and you want to _____."

PHASES OF HELPING

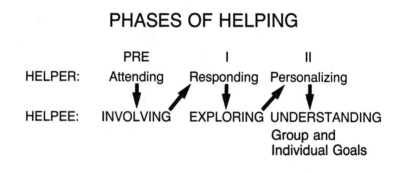

"You feel disappointed in yourselves because you can't handle this course and you're eager to learn how to do so. On the other hand, she feels disappointed because she can't succeed for her own purposes and she wants to learn to be her own person."

UNDERSTANDING GROUP GOALS

Also, in initiating, the helpers initiate with both the individuals and the group as a whole. The helpers help to
define goals and develop programs with both individuals
and the groups. In so doing they use the format for communicating goals and program steps: "Your goal is
_____ as indicated by _____. Your first step is
_____."

PHASES OF HELPING

	PRE	I	II	III
HELPER:	Attending	Responding	Personalizing	Initiating
HELPEE:	INVOLVING	EXPLORING	UNDERSTANDING	ACTING Upon Group and Individual Programs

"Your goal is to manage this course as indicated by a pass-ing grade. For your first step, we'll put together a little group for learning-how-to-learn this content."

"Her goal is to become in-dependent of her parents' wishes. Her first step is to enter into our "dealing up" skills training group."

ACTING UPON GROUP PROGRAMS

We recycle in groups in the same manner as with individuals—exploring, understanding and acting with the group as a whole as well as with individuals within the group. Thus, as the group members act, they recycle the feedback from their action to stimulate more extensive action. If, for example, the group is unsure of its next topic or future direction, then they might recycle exploring, understanding and acting upon developing and implementing a preferred course of action. If the group considers various skills training programs, then they might recycle consideration of group training as a preferred mode of helping.

PHASES OF HELPING

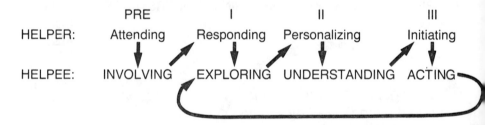

RECYCLING IN GROUPS

Applying Helping Skills to Teaching as Treatment

Just as group processes are a preferred mode of helping, so are "teaching as treatment (TAT)" processes a
preferred mode of group helping. TAT emphasizes
teaching helpees the skills they need to help themselves.
Again, TAT is most effective in a group context yet also
highly desirable on an individual basis. TAT produces ex-
emplary helpee outcomes by transforming helpee skill
deficits into skill assets.

The ingredients of TAT are related to helpee processing: preparing the content for the helpees facilitates
helpee involvement; diagnosing the helpees facilitates
helpee exploring; setting goals with the helpees facilitates
helpee understadning; and programming with the
helpees facilitates helpee action.

TEACHING AS TREATMENT —
A PREFERRED MODE OF HELPING

During the pre-helping phase, the helpers attended to the helpees in order to involve them in helping. Now a new ingredient is introduced—the teaching content. The content will teach the helpees skills in their deficit areas. For example, the content may teach them: interpersonal skills in relating to their parents or the opposite sex; learning skills in different content areas; or working skills in different working contexts. Therefore, the helpers need to prepare the content for their helpees just as I prepared this book for its readers. The helpers must not only develop and organize the skills and knowledge and the methods to teach them. They must also relate the skills content to the helpees' frames of reference. In so doing, they are preparing the content for involving the helpees in the TAT learning process.

PHASES OF HELPING

	PRE
HELPER:	Attending
	&
	Preparing
	↓
HELPEE:	INVOLVING

PREPARING FOR HELPEES

With the introduction of teaching content, the helpers must proceed simultaneously along two tracks: one internal and one external. The helpees' internal frames of reference are addressed by the helpers' responsiveness. The content's external frame of reference is addressed by the helpers' diagnosing. Just as the helpers responded to the helpees' internal frames of reference, so do they now respond to the external frame of reference of the content: they diagnose the helpees in terms of their skill and knowledge levels. Thus, they facilitate the helpees' exploring where they are with the learning experience from both internal and external frames of reference. In so doing, the helpers continue to use the format for responding to feeling and meaning.

PHASES OF HELPING

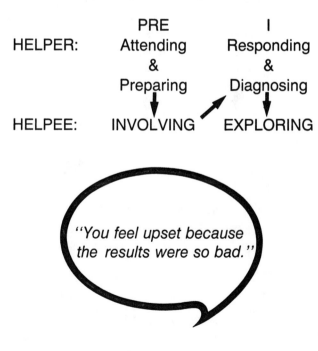

	PRE	I
HELPER:	Attending & Preparing	Responding & Diagnosing
HELPEE:	INVOLVING	EXPLORING

"You feel upset because the results were so bad."

EXPLORING SKILL DEFICITS

Similarly, with the diagnosis available, the helpers may proceed to set goals with the helpees from the external frame of reference of the content. The helpers work with the helpees to develop goals based upon the diagnosis of the helpees' skill and knowledge levels. Again, usually the goals are the skill steps or skill level that the helpees cannot perform satisfactorily, as well as any supportive knowledge that they may require to perform those steps. At the same time, the helpers personalize those goals from the internal frames of reference of the helpees. Thus, they facilitate the helpees' understanding of where they are in relation to where they want to be with the learning experience. In so doing, the helpers continue to use the format for personalizing problems and goals.

PHASES OF HELPING

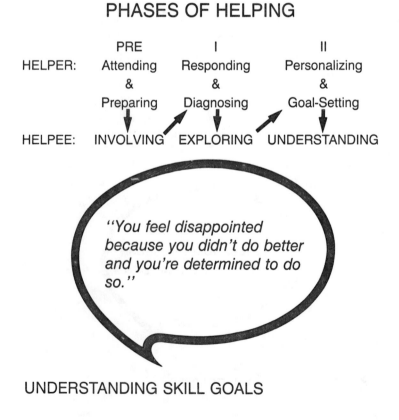

PRE   I   II

HELPER: Attending   Responding   Personalizing
     &   &   &
  Preparing   Diagnosing   Goal-Setting

HELPEE: INVOLVING   EXPLORING   UNDERSTANDING

"You feel disappointed because you didn't do better and you're determined to do so."

UNDERSTANDING SKILL GOALS

Finally, the helpers work with the helpees to develop programs to achieve the goals from the external frame of reference of the content. At the same time, the helpers work with the helpees to individualize and initiate the action programs from the helpees' internal frames of reference. The helpers work to define goals and develop programs in terms of both the helpees' needs (external) as well as the helpees' wants (internal). Thus, they facilitate the helpees' acting to get from where they are to where they want or need to be with the learning experience. In so doing, the helpers continue to use the format for communicating goals and program steps.

PHASES OF HELPING

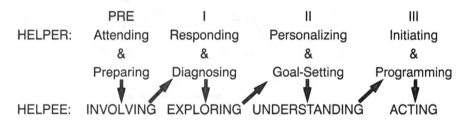

	PRE	I	II	III
HELPER:	Attending & Preparing	Responding & Diagnosing	Personalizing & Goal-Setting	Initiating & Programming
HELPEE:	INVOLVING	EXPLORING	UNDERSTANDING	ACTING

"Your goal is improving your performance as indicated by your test results. Your first step is to begin with the most immediate problem—taking tests."

ACTING UPON SKILL PROGRAMS

TAT is recycled in exactly the same manner as any other helping process. Helpee acting elicits feedback. Feedback stimulates further diagnosing and responding to explore. Exploring generates goal-setting and personalizing to understand. Understanding facilitates individualizing and initiating programs to act. Recycling continues in TAT as in life: it is directly related to growing. Indeed, they are one and the same: recycling processing and learning new skills define growing in life.

PHASES OF HELPING

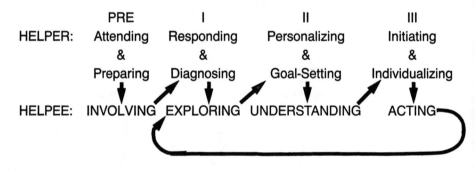

Summary

In recycling the helping process, we may want to conceptualize it in terms that will stay with us: attending, responding, understanding, acting. If we know how each of these helping skills relates to the phases of human processing, then we will never be lost in anything we do in life. Indeed, the critical incidents that are now crises for us become simply opportunities for recycling our skills.

LEVELS OF HELPING

5.0	Initiating
4.0	Personalizing
3.0	Responding
2.0	Attending
1.0	Nonattending

Going through the helping process once with a helpee may be an intense and fulfilling experience. But growth is not static. Growth is life-long processing. A growing person is constantly involved in processing in an ongoing, ever expanding spiral of life. This spiral emphasizes our purposeful effort to constantly improve our functioning and our contributions to the world.

PHASES OF HELPING

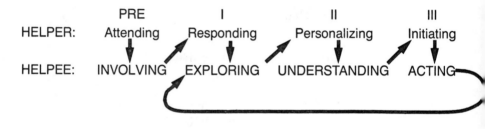

	PRE	I	II	III
HELPER:	Attending	Responding	Personalizing	Initiating
HELPEE:	INVOLVING	EXPLORING	UNDERSTANDING	ACTING

RECYCLING

You now know about recycling the helping process. You will want to practice these skills throughout your life in all living, learning and working situations.

Case Study #10—Skilled Helping

HELPEE PROCESSING/ HELPER RECYCLING	TYPE OF RESPONSE
Tom: "You know, I've tried to work things out with my parents. But things didn't work out the way I rehearsed them."	
Helper: "You're pretty upset because your rehearsals didn't pan out."	Responding to Meaning
Tom: "Yeah. Maybe I didn't check myself out while I was attending to them but I was really trying."	
Helper: "You're also upset because you left out a few key check steps."	Responding to Meaning
Tom: "Yeah. But I'm most disappointed in their reactions to me. I was really trying to attend to them. And they kept holding me off."	
Helper: "You're disappointed that they didn't receive your attentiveness."	Responding to Meaning
Tom: "Maybe they're just not ready for it. Or suspicious of it."	
Helper: "You're unsure because they may think you're only attentive to set them up for something bigger."	Responding to Meaning
Tom: "It's true. I often did set them up in the past. Maybe they're just not ready for a change in me."	

Helper:	"You're really sad because you're left out of their lives."	**Personalizing Meaning**
Tom:	"Maybe I'm not ready yet."	
Helper:	"You're really disappointed in yourself because you didn't bring it off with them."	**Personalizing the Problem**
Tom:	"They do mean so much to me."	
Helper:	"You're committed to working things through with them."	**Personalizing the Goal**
Tom:	"Yeah. I've revised my program and built in some more check steps. I'm going to make it work."	
Helper:	"You're determined to follow through with them. Maybe we need to work on a step that lets them know that you're really trying to change—to help them become attentive with you."	**Initiating a Program Step**
Tom:	"I just wish my parents could get into some listening instead of just yelling at me all the time."	
Helper:	"You're saying that your parents holler a lot and don't pay much attention to what you have to say."	**Responding to Content**
Joan:	"His parents and mine, too. Honestly, they treat us like we were little kids!"	
Helper:	"You feel pretty angry with them."	**Responding to Feeling**
Tom:	"They're living in a dream world."	

Helper:	"It bugs you that they're so out of touch."	**Responding to Meaining**
Joan:	"They don't even know that the real world today is a whole new thing!"	
Helper:	"You feel mad because they don't even know what's going on."	**Responding to Meaning**
Tom:	"I just wish they'd let up on us."	
Helper:	"You really resent that they're always on your back."	**Responding to Meaning**
Joan:	"We both do. See, we've been making some plans of our own. Only they won't believe that we're—I don't know—mature enough to handle things."	
Helper:	"It's frustrating when your parents don't accept your capability."	**Responding to Meaning**
Tom:	"You know it! I mean, all we want to do is live together. That's no big thing today, right? But they're such jerks, they think we're going to ruin our lives!"	
Helper:	"You feel furious because they won't let you make your own decisions."	**Responding to Meaning**
Joan:	"Exactly! We've tried to be responsible with them, but it hasn't helped. I don't know how we're supposed to convince them that we're, well, practically adults."	
Helper:	"What it comes down to is that you are both fed up with the fact	

that they want to keep you on a leash and you want to live your own lives on your own terms and not theirs."

Responding to Meaning

Tom: "It's really a messed-up situation any way you look at it."

Helper: "It's a lousy feeling because even though you're pretty mad at your parents, you still care a lot about how they feel."

Personalizing Meaning

Joan: "I—yeah, I've thought about that."

Tom: "Well, I guess I've probably had some questions myself. I mean, how could we help it when our parents are making us look at the bad side all the time?"

Helper: "So you're kind of uneasy, too, Tom, because you're not confident enough in yourself to be sure you are doing the right thing."

Personalizing Meaning

Joan: "It's like—well, when my parents tell me what to do, it makes me very defensive. But when I'm alone—I don't know—what if we went ahead and then found out we were making a mistake?"

Helper: "It concerns you because you can't figure out for sure what's the best thing for you both to do regardless of what others want you to do."

Personalizing the Problem

Tom:	"Uh huh. I mean—well, I love Joan too much to want to do something for the wrong reason—just to get back at my parents, for example."	
Helper:	"It's scary because you can't be sure you're doing the right thing for the right reasons."	**Personalizing the Feeling**
Joan:	"That's just it. I don't think we would even be so ready to live together if our parents weren't so set against it."	
Helper:	"You feel frightened because you can't stop living in reaction to your parents even though you want to make decisions that reflect who you are."	**Personalizing the Goal**
Tom:	"Yeah, we've got to be ourselves."	
Helper:	"You're certain you want to be yourselves even though you're sometimes not sure what that really means."	**Responding to Meaning**
Helper:	"It sounds to me like your goal isn't really to live together—but that you really want to find a way to make decisions based on your own values, rather than just re-acting to others. That really means being able to use your personal values to decide whether or not to live together."	**Defining the Goal**

Tom: "Yeah—but that's just it. Even when I know something is important, I can't seem to figure out what to do about it."

Helper: "It's irritating when you can't figure out how to live by your own values. The first thing you might do is explore your values and then make a list of all the things that are important to you." — Initiating the First Step

Joan: "Sure—but how's that going to help us know what to do?"

Helper: "Well, once you know what's important, you can prioritize your values by deciding which one is most important, next important, and so on—then you can use all this information to make the decision." — Initiating Intermediate Steps

Tom: "I get it—you mean some of our values ought to influence our decision more than others and we have to know that to make the best choice."

Helper: "That's right. When do you think you could make up a list of your values and priorities so we could get together again and talk them over?" — Initiating Schedules

Joan: "We can get that done this afternoon and tonight."

Helper: "O.K. If you do that, then I'll meet
with you both again on Thursday
to review what you've done and
to show you how to use those
values systematically to make the   **Initiating**
best choices for you."   **Reinforcement**

Tom: "I think we're going to feel a whole
lot better once we've worked this
thing through."

Helper: "You already feel a lot better just
knowing that you're going to be
able to make the best decision
based on the things that are really   **Responding**
important to you."   **to Meaning**

7
Summary and
Conclusions

Our only reason to live is to grow. Human processing is our vehicle to growth. We humans are the products of our processing. Indeed, we are only human when we are processing. In the end, we either die growing. Or we die like animals, conditioned and impotent, homeless in our own world.

Thus far we have concentrated upon the helping process. The helpers offer helping skills to the helpees. The helpees use these helping skills to engage in processing. The entire helping process is guided by the effectiveness of the helpees' movement through exploring, understanding and acting. The helpees emit the cues of their readiness to move from one phase to the next. The helpers facilitate this movement.

The helping process can be used for all problems and goals in living, learning and working. It can help us to resolve international crises between nations as well as to help our infants to survive or our students to learn or our employees to work. There is no human problem or goal too large or complex—not in space or on Earth. Helping is the universal process for achieving human ends.

HELPER

Process

HELPEE

Here is an illustration of helping people to deal with some of the kinds of concerns that may come to dominate humankind.

Floyd: "We're kind of angry with your . whole generation. You left us all the mess—and the pollution and garbage."

Helper: "You're saying that we've copped out on the problems and stuck you with them."

Responding to Content

Tom: "Yeah, my parents, you, all of you people that have been around but haven't done anything to set things straight."

Helper: "It really makes you angry."

Responding to Feeling

Joan: "Yeah, and a lot of you did more than that—you sold out for bucks!"

Helper: "You feel furious that a lot of us settled for a messed up world— for a price. I think a lot of us probably hung on to the idea that part of the price would be a better world for our kids—for you."

Responding to Meaning

Floyd: "Yeah, well maybe that's what you thought. But just look at the world you're getting ready to hand over to us."

Helper: "It's really frustrating for you because we sold out for the short-

range view and missed out com-
pletely on the long-range
conditions."

Responding
to Meaning

Joan: "You really blew it."

Helper: "You really resent what we've
done."

Responding
to Meaning

Tom: "Really! I mean, how are we supposed to act when the people who
are supposed to know better act
the way you all have?"

Helper: "You're sore because we're supposed to have the answers and yet
it's pretty obvious we don't."

Responding
to Meaning

Joan: "Yeah, sure, only now it sounds
like the whole load's on us!"

Helper: "It's frightening to have that
responsibility dumped on you."

Responding
to Meaning

Floyd: "And it isn't fair!"

Helper: "You're really upset about being
given the burden."

Responding
to Meaning

Tom: "Right."

Helper: "And you feel resentful toward me
for being part of it."

Immediacy

Joan: "Yeah, you're right. You are at
fault, but I guess all we've done so
far is make a lot of noise about
what's wrong. We really haven't
learned to do anything constructive
about it yet."

Helper: "You feel a little foolish because you haven't shown you can handle it any better than we have."   **Personalizing the Meaning**

Floyd: "And if we can't?"

Helper: "That makes me feel responsible because you're really asking if I can give you any help right now. And if I can't, then the implications are pretty heavy for all of us."   **Immediacy**

Tom: "It really does make a difference, knowing we're not alone. I guess we still need a lot of help."

Helper: "And it's frightening because you can't even figure out what it is you have to learn."   **Personalizing the Problem**

Joan: "Yeah, where do we begin?"

Helper: "You feel lost because you can't find a starting point."   **Personalizing the Feeling**

Tom: "Yeah, but there's still time for us."

Floyd: "We haven't really had our chance yet."

Helper: "Uh huh—you feel good that you still have a chance to make things better, but it also makes you anxious because you don't know how to begin making things better and you really want to succeed."   **Personalizing the Goal**

Joan: "We've got to succeed!"

Helper: "O.K. So the goal is to succeed where our generation has failed. What kind of things would indicate to you that you were succeeding?" **Personalizing the Goal**

Tom: "If there was less pollution."

Floyd: "A fair chance for women, blacks and other disenfranchised people."

Joan: "If there was more honesty in government and business."

Helper: "Those are big problems. Which one is most important?" **Defining the Goal**

Tom: "I think human rights has got to be number one."

Joan: "For sure."

Floyd: "Right. We ought to start right here with fair employment."

Helper: "That's a good place to start! But it's also a pretty big issue." **Defining the Goal**

Joan: "Yeah. Maybe we should tackle this one business at a time."

Helper: "You realize it's important to confront a big problem step-by-step. You can choose one major employer in the area to start with. How will you know when you've really make an impact?" **Defining the Goal**

Tom: "Good question—I sure don't know."

Floyd: "Well, don't they have some laws or guidelines about fair employment?"

Joan:	"Sure they do! I think they're called Equal Employment Opportunity Guidelines. We could use the guidelines to tell if a business is using fair employment practices."	
Helper:	"Good idea, Joan! Any idea how long that might take?"	**Defining the Goal**
Tom:	"That's hard to say, but I think by the end of six months we should be able to tell if we're on the right track or not."	
Helper:	"So you would believe that you had made a successful start if over the next six months you could bring at least one major employer in the area into compliance with the Equal Employment Opportunity Guidelines."	**Defining the Goal**
Tom:	"Great!"	
Floyd:	"I don't even know where to start."	
Helper:	"It's a big job. But one way you might begin would be to learn how to develop an effective action plan to get there."	**Initiating the First Step**
Joan:	"Right, then we'd have to develop skills, wouldn't we? So we could really figure out where we're going and how we're going to get there."	

Helper: "That's right. And by getting planning skills, you'd be able to plan
the other skills you'd need to
really attack the problem. Your   Initiating
actual plan of attack would repre-   Intermediate
sent another step."   Steps

Floyd: "Man, that'd be a whole lot better
than just complaining and moan-
ing and wasting a lot of energy!"

Helper: "It feels good to know you really
can approach even the toughest   Responding
problem in a systematic way."   to Meaning

Helper: "Another thing you can do is
make sure you work on at least
one new skill each week—and
then figure out a system of per-   Initiating
sonal rewards and punishments   Schedules &
depending on whether you ac-   Reinforce-
tually stay on schedule."   ments

Joan: "I think you're trying to show us it
really can be done—and I think
I'm beginning to believe you.

Helper: "Things look a whole lot brighter
when you begin to see that there   Responding
is something you can do to help!"   to Meaning

Facilitating Human Processing

Whether or not this or any other generation will make a difference for humankind depends upon whether or not they are transformed from helpees to helpers. We have devoted this book to the process in which the helpees must engage in order to learn to function effectively in their lives. The next step in becoming a helper is for us to acquire content steps and knowledge. These steps will enable us to perform the skills necessary to make a difference in our lives and worlds. For example, to become fully helpful, we must go on to acquire all of the skills content in this book as well as all of the living, learning and working skills content implied by the helping process.

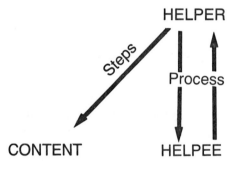

ACQUIRING SKILL STEPS

The next step to becoming a helper is to apply the skills
to certain objectives. In our lives, for example, we may
want to relate more effectively; to learn more efficiently
and effectively; and to work more productively. We must
practice applying the skills involved to our objectives in all
living, learning and working areas. Applying skills requires
the most practice because it prepares us for our real-life
skill transfers. The more variety in and between objectives, the greater the probability of being successful in our
real-life ventures. For example, we may practice applying
the helping skills by varying the components, functions,
processes, conditions or standards of the skills.

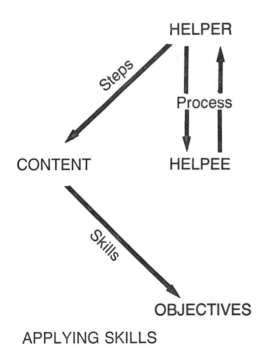

APPLYING SKILLS

The next step in our helper program is to transfer the skills we have acquired and applied to our real-life contexts. Thus, we transfer to relate more effectively to our loved ones and friends; to learn more efficiently and effectively in school or in training; to work more productively at work; or, indeed, to play more recreationally at play. We may learn to transfer all skills creatively by changing one or more of the components, functions, processes, conditions or standards while holding the others constant. For example, we may attend to a policeman on the road or a judge in traffic court to facilitate productive processing by changing the components and conditions.

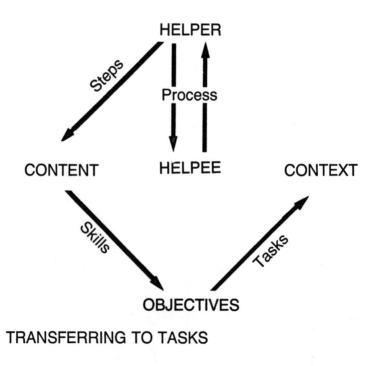

TRANSFERRING TO TASKS

The final step in becoming a helper is to master the achievement of all our goals. These goals include our rehabilitative goals as well as our preventative goals. Thus, for example, we may become more effective with people in our lives. We may accomplish higher levels of achievement in our educational endeavors. We may become more cost beneficial in our efforts at work.

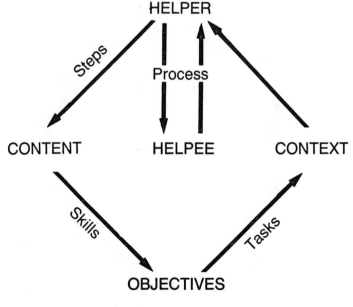

MASTERING GOALS

Ultimately, we cannot be productive until we can help others to achieve their goals. This means that we can design programs to intervene productively in the lives of others. We do this by working with others to accomplish the following: 1) establishing productive goals; 2) assessing the contextual tasks needed to achieve the goals; 3) specifying the skill objectives needed to perform the tasks; 4) developing the skill steps content needed to achieve the objectives; 5) delivering the process needed to learn the skill steps. Again, this process is recycled as we assess the degree to which our recipients process, acquire, apply and transfer their skills and achieve their goals.

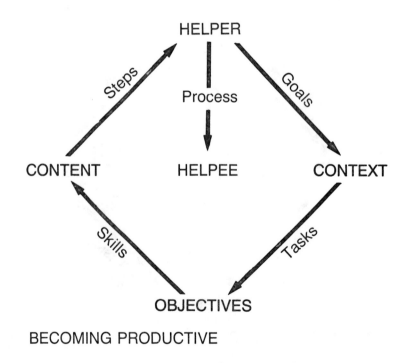

BECOMING PRODUCTIVE

We may use our helping skills to resolve any human problems and achieve any human goals. We may put a person on the moon or educate a child in a classroom. Any goal that we can conceive, we can operationalize. Any goal that we can operationalize, we can achieve.

The great irony is that, in the process of becoming programmatic and productive, we also become human. It is only in the use of our intellects to process our experience that we discover our humanity. It is only in the use of our intellects to process to achieve human goals that we demonstrate our humanity.

Humankind's goals in space or on Earth are limited only by the power of our processing. Humanity defines itself by its ability to facilitate this processing—in ourselves and others.

BECOMING HUMAN

Appendices

APPENDIX A

FEELING WORD LIST*

Excited	Surprised	Happy	Satisfied
alive	amazed	blissful	agreeable
animated	astonished	captivated	appeased
charged	astounded	cheerful	assuaged
delirious	awed	ecstatic	charmed
eager	bewildered	elated	contented
energized	dazed	enraptured	delighted
great	dumbfounded	exalted	enchanted
intoxicated	flabbergasted	excellent	enjoyment
roused	floored	exuberant	fulfilled
stimulated	jarred	fantastic	glad
stirred	jolted	grand	good
thrilled	nonplussed	great	gratified
titillated	overcome	heavenly	nice
	rocked	incredible	pleasant
	shaken	jolly	pleased
	shocked	joyful	pleasurable
	speechless	lively	sated
	staggered	magnificent	satiated
	startled	overflowing	
	stunned	spirited	
	stupefied	special	
	thunderstruck	splendid	
		super	
		tickled	
		terrific	
		triumphant	
		wild	
		wonderful	

*This list is in alphabetical order by feeling category. Since the intensity of any feeling word depends upon the person with whom it is used, you will need to visualize the typical helpee you work with to categorize these works by intensity level.

Appreciative	Affectionate	Relieved	Calm
admire	affectionate	allayed	bland
adore	attached	at ease	collected
apprise	attracted	comforted	composed
cherish	close	consoled	controlled
esteem	committed	freed	cool
grateful	devoted	helped	lulled
prize	enamored	refreshed	mellow
regard	endeared	rested	pacified
relish	fond	solaced	patient
respect	infatuated	soothed	peaceful
revere	like	unburdened	quiescent
thankful	love		quiet
treasure	rapture		relaxed
value	respect		reposed
	sentimental		restful
	sincere		sedated
	tenderness		serene
	warm		soothed
			staid
			still
			undisturbed
			unruffled

Distressed	Frightened	Anxious	Sad
afflicted	afraid	agitated	awful
agony	aghast	baffled	bummed out
anguish	alarmed	blocked	despair
annoyed	apprehensive	careful	devastated
bad	cautious	confounded	disconsolate
bothered	dread	deterred	doleful
concerned	fear	disorganized	down
crushed	fearful	distracted	gloomy
discomfort	frantic	disturbed	grieved
distraught	hesitant	edgy	low
galled	intimidated	flighty	melancholy
hurt	panicky	hassled	miserable
ill at ease	petrified	hindered	mournful
indisposed	scared	inhibited	pitiful
injured	shakey	jittery	shattered
miserable	spooked	muddled	somber
pained	startled	nervous	sorrowful
sick	terrified	overwhelmed	sorry
suffering	threatened	perplexed	sullen
tormented	trepidation	restless	unhappy
troubled		stressed	woebegone
upset		tangled	
		tense	
		uncertain	
		uneasy	
		uptight	
		vigilant	
		worried	

Angry	Disgusted	Ashamed	Embarrassed
aggravated	abhorred	blameworthy	abashed
antipathy	abominated	chagrined	awkward
annoyed	averse	condemnable	demeaned
bitter	degraded	contrite	discomfited
bristle	demoralized	criminal	discomforted
bugged	dismayed	deceitful	disconcerted
chafed	evil	delinquent	dumb
crabby	gross	derelict	flustered
cranky	horrified	dishonest	foolish
displeased	nauseated	guilty	meek
enraged	noxious	humiliated	put down
frustrated	offended	mortified	rattled
fuming	repelled	regretful	red-faced
furious	repugnant	remorse	self-conscious
hateful	repulsed	repentive	scapegoated
hostile	revolted	reprehensible	shy
indignant	revulsion	shame	silly
inflamed	rotten	sheepish	stupid
infuriated	sickened	sinful	uncomfortable
irate	vile	worthless	withdrawn
irked	wicked		
livid			
mad			
outraged			
peeved			
perturbed			
piqued			
rankled			
resentful			
riled			
sore			
steamed			
ticked off			
worked up			

APPENDIX B

THE EVOLUTION OF THE HELPING MODEL

In the early 1960's, a number of challenges were issued to the helping professions (Eysenck, 1960, 1965; Levitt, 1963; Lewis, 1965). These challenges stated that counseling and psychotherapy did not make a difference. They discovered that both adults and children who were in control groups, gained as much, on the average, as people assigned to professional counselors and therapists; about two-thirds of the patients improved and remained out of the hospital a year after treatment, whether they were treated or not.

This research was updated in longitudinal studies of more than 50 treatment settings by Anthony (1979). He studied the lasting effects of counseling, rehabilitation and psychotherapeutic techniques. He found that, within three to five years after treatment, 65 to 75 percent of the ex-patients were once again patients. Also, regardless of the follow-up period, the gainful employment of ex-patients was below 25 percent.

The major conclusion that might be drawn from these data is that counseling and psychotherapy—as traditionally practiced—are effective in about 20 percent of the cases. (Of the two-thirds of the clients and patients who eventually get better, only one-third to one quarter stay better. This means that psychotherapy has lasting positive effects in 17 to 22 percent of the cases.) To answer these challenges, further research was undertaken. We will examine the naturalistic studies of helping that led to predictive studies and, in turn, to the generalization and extension of an effective helping skills model.

NATURALISTIC STUDIES

One answer to the challenges to helping came from studying the natural variability of the professionally-treated groups. The clients and patients of professional helpers demonstrated a greater range of effects than those in professionally "untreated" groups (Rogers et al., 1967; Truax and Carkhuff, 1967). This meant that professional practitioners tended to have a greater spread of effects on their patients; some got significantly better and some got worse. This finding suggested one very consoling conclusion: counseling and psychotherapy really did make a difference. It also suggested one very distressing conclusion: counseling and psychotherapy have a two-edged effect—they may be helpful or harmful (Bergin and Garfield, 1971).

Furthermore, the truly significant finding was that you could account, at least in part, for these helpful, neutral and harmful effects. The effects could be determined by the levels of functioning of the helpers on certain interpersonal dimensions such as empathy or empathic understanding. Counselors and therapists who offered high levels of a certain core of interpersonal dimensions facilitated the process and outcome of their clients and patients while clients and patients of helpers offering low levels of understanding stayed the same or were retarded in their process and outcome (Rogers et al., 1967; Truax and Carkhuff, 1967).

PREDICTIVE STUDIES

Following these early naturalistic studies, a number of predictive validity studies were conducted. These involved manipulating the levels of the helper's functioning on interpersonal dimensions such as empathy. The effects of these manipulations were studied both within the helping process and upon the helping outcomes. In general, within the helping process, the helpees (clients and patients) changed according to the helper's level of functioning: when the helpers offered high levels of interpersonal dimensions such as empathy, the helpees explored their problems in meaningful ways. When the helpers offered low levels of interpersonal dimensions, the helpees did not explore their problems in meaningful ways (Carkhuff and Alexik, 1967; Holder et al., 1967; Piaget et al., 1968; Truax and Carkhuff, 1967).

In the studies of helping outcomes, it was found that the helpees moved in the direction of the helpers' levels of functioning. In general, helpees of helpers functioning at high levels of these interpersonal dimensions moved toward higher levels of functioning. Helpees of helpers functioning at low levels of these interpersonal dimensions moved toward lower levels of functioning (Pagell et al., 1967)

GENERALIZATION STUDIES

The next series of studies sought to generalize the effects of these interpersonal dimensions to other helping and human relationships. The first effort was to study the effects of teachers' levels of interpersonal functioning upon learners' development. Aspy and Roebuck (1972) divided teachers into high and low levels of interpersonal functioning and found significant relationships with student achievement indices such as Word Meaning, Paragraph Meaning, Spelling, Word Study Skills and Language. A number of subsequent studies were conducted assessing the relationship of interpersonal dimensions with a variety of other student outcome indices: the students of teachers offering high levels of these interpersonal dimensions demonstrated significant constructive gains in areas of emotional, interpersonal, and intellectual functioning (Aspy and Roebuck, 1977).

These effects have been generalized in all areas of helping and human relationships where the "more knowing" person influences the "less knowing" person: parent-child relations (Carkhuff, 1971a; Carkhuff and Pierce, 1976); teacher-student relations (Aspy and Roebuck, 1977; Carkhuff, 1969); counselor-client relations (Berenson and Carkhuff, 1967; Carkhuff and Berenson, 1967); and therapist-patient relations (Anthony, 1979; Rogers et al., 1967; Truax and Carkhuff, 1967). In general, the "less knowing" persons will move toward the levels of functioning of the "more knowing" persons over time, depending on both the extensiveness and intensity of contacts: helpees of high-level functioning helpers get better on a variety of process and outcome indices, while helpees of low-level functioning helpers get worse.

EXTENSION STUDIES

Finally, a number of studies were conducted to extend the dimensions of helping. For example, Vitalo (1970) found that the effects of behavior modification programs were contingent, in part, upon the modifiers' levels of interpersonal functioning. Mickelson and Stevic (1971) found that career information-seeking behavior was dependent upon the helpers' levels of interpersonal functioning in interaction with their reinforcement programs. In general, those helpers who functioned at the highest levels, and had the most systematic helping programs, were most effective in helping their helpees.

Simultaneously, the core interpersonal dimensions were gradually extended and then factored into responsive and initiative dimensions (Berenson and Mitchell, 1974; Carkhuff, 1969). (Responsive dimensions respond to the helpee's experience. Initiative dimensions, while taking into consideration the helpee's experience, are generated from the helper's experience.) In addition, a number of systematic helping programs were developed to extend the helper's initiative activities to culminate in effective action programs for the helpees (Carkhuff, 1969, 1971a).

In summary, those helping dimensions that appear naturally in a limited number of effective helpers were validated in predictive studies of both helping process and outcome. In addition, the effectiveness of these helping dimensions was generalized to all helping and human relationships. Finally, these dimensions were extended to equip the helpers with more of the ingredients they needed to effectively help others. The acceptance of these fundamental ingredients of helping has been widely demonstrated in the professional literature (Brammer, 1979; Combs et al., 1978; Danish and Hauer, 1973; Egan, 1975; Gazda, 1973; Gordon, 1975; Hackney and Cornier, 1979; Johnson, 1972; Okun, 1976; Patterson, 1973).

THE EVOLUTION OF THE DIMENSIONS

Over a period of time, the core dimensions of helping have evolved and have been extended in a never-ending attempt to account for helping effectiveness. What began with a gross definition of the dimension of empathy, has evolved into an extensive equation for human resource development. In order to understand these dimensions, we must understand four things: the sources of helping dimensions as well as their evolution; the helping process which these dimensions impact; the helper skills which operationalize the dimensions; and the helpee outcomes which these dimensions are intended to achieve.

HELPING SOURCES

There are two fundamental approaches to helping. One may be called the insight approach. The other may be conceived of as the action approach. The insight approach has been supported by many traditional therapeutic schools. In particular, the psychoanalytic, neoanalytic and client-centered practitioners have emphasized the client's insight as the basis for the development of an effective set of assumptions about his or her world (Adler, 1927; Freud, 1933; Fromm, 1947; Horney, 1945; Jung, 1939; Rank, 1929; Rogers et al., 1967; Sullivan, 1948). The action approach has been promulgated by the learning theory and behavior modification schools as well as the trait-and-factor school, which matches people to jobs and vice versa. These schools have emphasized the client's development and implementation of rational action plans for managing his or her world (Eysenck, 1960; Ginzberg et al., 1951; Krasner and Ullman, 1965; Parsons, 1909; Super, 1949; Watson, 1916; Wolpe et al., 1964).

Unfortunately, both the insight and action approaches are incomplete without the other. Most insight approaches fail to develop the insights programmatically so that the client can "own" them. Even when they do, they fail to systematically develop action programs flowing from these insights. Similarly, while the action approaches develop their programs effectively, they fail to consolidate whatever behavior changes they have accomplished. They neglect to complement the action with insights so that the client can guide his or her own life (Carkhuff and Berenson, 1976, 1977). In order to effectively help human beings to change behavior, the insight and action approaches must be integrated into one effective helping process.

HELPING PROCESS

In order to demonstrate a change or gain in behavior, the helpees must act differently from the way they did before. In order to act effectively, the helpees must have insights or understand accurately their goals and the ways to achieve them. In order to understand their goals, the helpees must explore their world experientially. These three learning or relearning processes are the phases of helping through which the helpees must be guided (Carkhuff and Berenson, 1976).

The helpees must first explore where they are in relation to their worlds and the significant people in their worlds. They must next understand where they are in relation to where they want to be. Finally, they must act to get from where they are to where they want to be. With the feedback from their action, they can recycle the learning process for more extensive exploration, more accurate understanding and more effective action (Carkhuff and Berenson, 1976).

HELPER SKILLS

In order to be effective in helping, then, the helper skills must facilitate the helpee's movement through the three-way helping process. The historic dimension of empathy was complemented by unconditional positive regard and genuineness (Rogers et al., 1967). These dimensions were transformed by more operational definitions into accurate empathy, respect and genuineness (Carkhuff, 1969; Truax and Carkhuff, 1967). They were, in turn, complemented by other dimensions including specificity or concreteness, self-disclosure, confrontation, and immediacy and then factored into responsive and initiative dimensions (Berenson and Mitchell, 1974; Carkhuff, 1969).

The responsive dimensions (empathy, respect, specificity of expression) responded to the helpee's experience and,

thus, facilitated the helpee's movement toward understanding. The initiative dimensions (genuineness, self-
disclosure, confrontation, immediacy and concreteness) were
generated from the helper's experience and stimulated the
helpee's movement toward action (Berenson and Mitchell,
1974; Carkhuff, 1971a). These initiative dimensions were
later extended to incorporate the problem-solving skills and
program development skills needed to fully help the helpees
to achieve appropriate outcomes (Carkhuff, 1974b, 1975;
Carkhuff and Anthony, 1979).

HELPEE OUTCOMES

In the early research, the helpee outcomes emphasized the
emotional changes or gains of the helpees. Since the helping
methods were insight-oriented, the process emphasized
helpee exploration, and the outcome assessments measured
the changes in the helpee's level of emotional insights
(Rogers et al., 1967; Truax and Carkhuff, 1967). Clearly,
these emotional outcomes were restrictive because they were
assessing only one dimension of the helpee's functioning.

These outcomes were later defined more broadly to incorporate all dimensions of human resource development to
which the helping process is dedicated. The emotional
dimension was extended to incorporate the interpersonal
functioning of the helpees (Carkhuff, 1969, 1971a). The
dimension of physical functioning was added to measure
relevant data on the helpees' fitness and energy levels
(Collingwood, 1972). The intellectual dimension was added to
measure the helpees' intellectual achievement and capabil-
ities (Aspy and Roebuck, 1972, 1977).

In summary, helping effectiveness is a function of the
helper's skills to facilitate the helping process to accomplish
helping outcomes. Helping outcomes include the physical,
emotional and intellectual dimensions of human resource
development. The helping process, by which outcomes are
accomplished, emphasizes the helpee's exploration, understanding and acting. The helping skills, by which the process
is facilitated, include responding and initiating skills.

THE HELPING SKILLS

The responsive and initiative factors of helping dominate the helping process. They facilitate the exploration, understanding and action that culminate in the physical, emotional and intellectual helpee outcomes. As a result of attempts to teach helpers how to accomplish these processes and outcomes, the responsive and initiative dimensions were further refined into concrete helping skills. These helping skills are called attending, responding, personalizing and initiating. The attending skills are preparatory to responding and the personalizing skills are transitional between responding and initiating.

ATTENDING SKILLS

Attending skills involve communicating a "hovering attentiveness" to the helpee. By attending physically, the helper communicates interest in the helpee's welfare. By observing and listening, the helper learns from and about the helpee. Attending is the richest source of learning about the helpee (Barker, 1971; Birdwhistell, 1967; Ekman et al., 1972; Garfield, 1971; Genther and Moughan, 1977; Genther and Sacuzzo, 1977; Hall, 1959, 1976; Ivey and Authier, 1971, 1978; Mehrabian, 1972; Schefflen, 1969; Smith-Hanen, 1977).

Within the helping process, attending serves to facilitate the helpee's involvement in helping. By communicating interest in the helpee, the helper establishes the conditions for the helpee's involvement in the helping process. Reduced to their minimum, attending skills may be seen as the acts of being decent to the helpee in a world that is very often indecent (Carkhuff and Berenson, 1976).

RESPONDING SKILLS

Basic responding skills involve the helper's accurate understanding of the helpee's experience. They include first discriminating and then communicating the content and feelings of the helpee's experience. When employed at levels interchangeable with the helpee's experience, they serve to insure that the helper is fully in tune with the helpee (Aspy and Roebuck, 1977; Carkhuff, 1969; Carkhuff and Berenson, 1967, 1977; Rogers et al., 1967; Truax and Carkhuff, 1967).

Responding skills serve to stimulate the helpee's exploration of where he or she is in his or her experience of the world. The accurate response becomes a mirror image of the helpee's experience. Responding skills also serve to reinforce the helpee's exploration by showing the helpee that the helper is fully in tune with the helpee's experience (Carkhuff and Berenson, 1976).

PERSONALIZING SKILLS

Personalizing skills involve responding to the personal implications of the meaning, problem, feeling and, finally, the goal. The helper processes the learning from helpee exploration and initiates movement toward understanding through a consideration of personalized implications. Personalizing skills culminate in the helpee's personal experience of the problem as the inability to handle difficult situations (Adler, 1927; Anthony, 1971; Berenson and Mitchell, 1974; Binswanger, 1956; Carkhuff, 1969; Carkhuff and Berenson, 1976; Freud, 1933; Fromm, 1947; Heidegger, 1962; Horney, 1945, Jung, 1939; May, 1961; Rank, 1929; Sullivan, 1948).

Personalizing skills are used to provide a transition from responding to initiating and from exploring to acting. When employed effectively, they facilitate the helpee's understanding of where he or she wants to be in the world. They serve to focus upon the helpee's goals which are the basis for acting (Carkhuff and Berenson, 1976).

INITIATING SKILLS

Finally, initiating skills involve operationalizing the goals, and then developing and implementing the steps to achieve these goals. Again, remember that the goals are calculated to resolve the helpee's problems. Most simply, initiative skills foster the development and implementation of the mechanical steps that are required to achieve the personalized goals that the helpee has developed (Authier et al., 1975; Carkhuff, 1969, 1971b, 1974b, 1975; Carkhuff and Anthony, 1979; Collingwood et al., 1978; Goldstein et al., 1976; Ivey, 1976;

Sprinthall and Mosher, 1971).

The initiating skills conclude the first cycle of the helping process. The helper employs initiative skills to stimulate the helpee's acting to achieve his or her goals. When employed effectively, initiative skills facilitate the helpee's acting to get to where he or she wants to be in the world (Carkhuff and Berenson, 1976).

In summary: the attending skills serve to involve the helpee in helping; responding skills facilitate exploration; personalizing skills facilitate understanding; and initiating skills stimulate acting. Again, with the feedback from acting, the helping or learning process is recycled until the goals are achieved.

THE TRAINING APPLICATIONS

It was a natural step to train helpers in helping skills and study the effects on helping outcomes. Indeed, the development of both the skills technologies and the training sytems was a highly interactional process, with each refining the other and both, in turn, being shaped by their outcomes. It was also only natural that the first of these training applications take place with credentialed counselors and therapists. Next came the training of lay and indigenous helper populations, followed by the direct training of helpee populations to service themselves.

CREDENTIALED HELPERS

The first series of training applications demonstrated that professional helpers could be trained to function at levels commensurate with "outstanding" practitioners (Truax & Carkhuff, 1967). In a later series, it was established that credentialed professionals could, in the brief time of 100 hours or less, learn to function above minimally effective and self-sustaining levels of interpersonal skills, levels beyond those offered by most "outstanding" practitioners (Carkhuff, 1969). Perhaps most importantly, trained counselors were able to involve their counselees in the helping process at levels that led to constructive change or gain. In one demonstration study in guidance, against a very low base success rate of 13 to 25 percent, the trained counselors were able to demonstrate success rates between 74 and 91 percent (Carkhuff and Berenson, 1976).

A series of training applications in teaching soon followed. Hefele (1971) found student achievement to be a function of systematic training of teachers in helping skills. Berenson (1971) found the experimentally-trained teachers were rated significantly higher in interpersonal skills and competency in the classroom than were other teachers who received a variety of control conditions (including a training control group, a Hawthorne Effect control group and a control group proper). Aspy and Roebuck (1977), building upon their earlier work, have continued to employ a variety of teacher training strategies demonstrating the positive effects of helping skills upon student physical, emotional and intellectual functioning.

FUNCTIONAL PROFESSIONALS

It is clear that a dimension such as interpersonal functioning is not the exclusive province of credentialed professionals. Lay personnel can learn as well as professionals to be caring and empathic in their relations with helpee populations. With this growing recognition, a number of training applications using lay personnel were conducted. The majority of these programs dealt with staff personnel.

Staff personnel, such as nurses and hospital attendants, policemen and prison guards, dormitory counselors and community volunteers, were trained and their effects in treatment studied. The effects were very positive for both the staff and helpee populations for, after all, the line staff and helpee populations were those who lived most intimately with each other. In general, the lay helpers were able to elicit significant changes in work behaviors, discharge rates, recidivism rates and a variety of other areas including self-reports, significant-other-reports and expert-reports (Carkhuff, 1969, 1971a; Carkhuff and Berenson, 1976).

INDIGENOUS PERSONNEL

The difference between functional professional staff and indigenous functional professionals is the difference between the attendant and the patient, the policeman and the delinquent, the guard and the inmate, and the teacher and the student. That is to say, indigenous personnel are part of the community being serviced. It is a natural extension of the lay helper training principle to train helpee recipients as well as staff.

Here the research indicates that, with systematic selection and training, indigenous functional professionals can work effectively with the populations from which they are drawn. For example, human relations specialists drawn from recipient ranks have facilitated school and work adjustments for troubled populations. New careers teachers, themselves drawn from the ranks of the unemployed, have systematically helped others to learn the skills they needed in order to get and hold meaningful jobs (Carkhuff, 1971a).

HELPEE POPULATIONS

The logical culmination of helper training is to train helpee populations directly in the kinds of skills which they need to service themselves. Thus, parents of emotionally disturbed children were systematically trained in the skills which they needed to function effectively with themselves and their children (Carkhuff and Bierman, 1970). Patients were trained to offer each other rewarding human relationships. The results were significantly more positive than all other forms of treatment, including individual or group therapy, drug treatment or "total push" treatment (Pierce and Drasgow, 1969). Training was, indeed, the preferred mode of treatment!

The concept of training as treatment led directly to the development of programs to train entire communities to create a therapeutic milieu. This has been accomplished most effectively in institutional-type settings where staff and residents are trained in the kinds of skills necessary to work effectively with each other. Thus both institutional and community-based criminal justice settings have yielded data indicating reduced recidivism and increased employability (Carkhuff, 1974a; Collingwood et al., 1978; Montgomery and Brown, 1980).

In summary, both lay staff and indigenous personnel may be selected and trained as functional professional helpers. In these roles, they can effect any human resource development—that professionals can—and more! Further, teaching the helpee populations the kinds of skills which they need to service themselves is a direct extension of the helper principle. When we train people in the skills which they need to function effectively in their worlds, we increase the probability that they will, in fact, begin to live, learn and work in increasingly constructive ways.

RESEARCH SUMMARY

The research of helping skills demonstrations over the last two decades is summarized in Tables 1 and 2. As can be seen in Table 1, 164 studies of 158,940 recipients are involved. The studies are divided as to their sources of effect—the effects of trained helpers or the effects of training helpees directly. In turn, the effects upon helpees are demonstrated in living, learning and working areas of functioning.

As can be seen in Table 2, the studies of the effects of helpers upon helpees are 96 percent positive while the indices are 92 percent positive. This means that various helpers—parents, counselors, teachers, employers—have constructive effects upon their helpees—children, counselees, students, employees—when trained in interpersonally-based helping skills. As can also be seen in Table 2, the studies of the direct effects of training the helpees are also 96 percent positive while the indices are 92 percent positive. This means that trained helpees—children, counselees, students, employees—demonstrate constructive change or gain when trained in interpersonally-based self-helping skills.

Overall, the studies of the effects of both helpers and direct training upon helpees are 96 percent positive while the indices are 92 percent positive. This means that our chances of achieving any reasonable living, learning or working outcome are about 95 percent when either helpers or helpees are training in interpersonally-based helping skills. Conversely, the chances of achieving any human goal without trained helpers or helpees are random.

CONCLUSIONS

In summary, training in interpersonal skills-based helping programs significantly increases the chances of our being effective in improving indices of helpee living, learning or working. Simply stated, trained helpers effectively elicit and use the input and feedback from the helpees concerning their helping effectiveness. Similarly, trained helpees learn to deal up, down and sideways in developing their own goals and programs.

We have found that all helping and human relationships may be "for better or for worse." The effects depend upon the helper's level of skills in facilitating the helpee's movement through the helping process toward constructive helping outcomes. These responsive and initiative helping skills constitute the core of all helping experiences.

The helping skills may be used in all one-to-one and one-to-group relationships. They are used in conjunction with the helper's specialty skills in counseling, teaching and working. They may be used in conjunction with any of a number of potential preferred modes of treatment, drawn from a variety of helping orientations, to meet the helpee's needs. Finally, the same skills may be taught directly to the helpees in order to help them help themselves: teaching clients skills is the preferred mode of treatment for most helpee populations.

In conclusion, the helping skills will enable us to have helpful rather than harmful effects upon the people with whom we relate. We can learn to become effective helpers with success rates ranging upwards from two-thirds to over 90 percent, against a base success rate of around 20 percent. Most importantly, we can use these skills to help ourselves and others to become healthy human beings and to form healthy human relationships.

TABLE 1.

An Index of Tables for the Studies of Recipient Living,
Learning and Working Outcomes

SOURCES OF EFFECT

Outcome Areas	Helpers	Helpees
Living	Table 2 (22 Studies) 25,682 Helpees	Table 6 (35 Studies) 2,279 Helpees
Learning	Tables 3 & 4 (32 Studies) 81,228 Learners	Table 7 (26 Studies) 3,610 Learners
Working	Table 5 (22 Studies) 33,836 Employees	Table 8 (27 Studies) 12,235 Employees
Sub-Totals	(76 Studies) 140,816 Recipients	(88 Studies) 18,124 Recipients
Grand Total	(164 Studies) 158,940 Recipients	

TABLE 2.

A Summary Index of Percentages of Predominantly
Positive Results of IPS Studies and Indices of Helpee
Living, Learning, and Working Outcomes

OUTCOMES	HELPERS	HELPEES	
LIVING (Table 2)			(Table 6)
Studies (N = 22)	91% Positive	91% Positive	Studies (N = 35)
Indices (N = 114)	83% Positive	85% Positive	Indices (N = 128)
LEARNING (Tables 3 & 4)			(Table 7)
Studies (N = 32)	97% Positive	100% Positive	Studies (N = 26)
Indices (N = 261)	92% Positive	99% Positive	Indices (N = 78)
WORKING (Table 5)			(Table 8)
Studies (N = 22)	100% Positive	100% Positive	Studies (N = 27)
Indices (N = 81)	96% Positive	98% Positive	Indices (N = 107)
SUB-TOTAL			
Studies (N = 76)	96% Positive	96% Positive	Studies (N = 88)
Indices (N = 456)	92% Positive	92% Positive	Indices (N = 313)
GRAND TOTAL			
Studies (N = 164)	96% Positive		
Indices (N = 769)	92% Positive		

REFERENCES

Adler, A. *Understanding Human Nature.* New York: Wolfe & Greenberg Publishers, 1927.

Anthony, W.A. A methodological investigation of the "minimally facilitative level of interpersonal function." *Journal of Clinical Psychology,* 1971, 27, 156-57.

Anthony, W.A. *The Principles of Psychiatric Rehabilitation.* Baltimore, Md.: University Park Press, 1979.

Aspy, D.N., and Roebuck, F.N. An investigation of the relationship between levels of cognitive functioning and the teacher's classroom behavior. *Journal of Educational Research,* May, 1972.

Aspy, D.N., and Roebuck, F.N. *KIDS Don't Learn From People They Don't Like.* Amherst, Mass.: Human Resource Development Press, 1977.

Authier, J. Gustafson, K., Guerney, B., and Kasdorf, J.A. The psychological practitioner as a teacher. *Counseling Psychologist,* 1975, 5, 31-50.

Bandler, R., and Grinder, J. *The Structure of Magic I & II.* Palo Alto, Cal: Science and Behavior Books, 1975.

Bandler, R., and Grinder, J. *Patterns of the Hypnotic Techniques of Milton H. Erickson, M.D.I.* Cupertino, Cal: Meta Publications, 1975.

Barker, L.L. *Listening Behavior.* Englewood Cliffs, N.J.: Prentice-Hall, 1971.

Berenson, B.G., and Carkhuff, R.R. *Sources of Gain in Counseling and Psychotherapy.* New York: Holt, Rinehart & Winston, 1967.

Berenson, B.G., and Mitchell, K.M. *Confrontation: For Better or Worse.* Amherst, Mass.: Human Resource Development Press, 1974.

Berenson, D.H. The effects of systematic human relations training upon the classroom performance of elementary school teachers. *Journal of Research and Development in Education,* 1971, 4, 70-85.

Bergin, A.E., and Garfield, S.L. (Eds.). *Handbook of Psychotherapy and Behavioral Change.* New York: John Wiley & Sons, 1971.

Binswanger, L. Existential analysis and psychotherapy. In F. Fromm-Reichmann and J.L. Moreno (Eds.), *Progress in Psychotherapy.* New York: Grune & Stratton, 1956.

Birdwhistell, R. Some body motion elements accompanying spoken American English. In L. Thayter (Ed.), *Communication: Concepts and Perspectives.* Washington, D.C.: Spartan, 1967.

Brammer, L. *The Helping Relationship. 2nd ed.* Englewood Cliffs, N.J.: Prentice-Hall, 1979.

Carkhuff, R.R. *Helping and Human Relations, Volumes I & II.* New York: Holt, Rinehart & Winston, 1969.

Carkhuff, R.R. *The Development of Human Resources.* New York: Holt, Rinehart & Winston, 1971 (a).

Carkhuff, R.R. Training as a preferred mode of treatment. *Journal of Counseling Psychology,* 1971 (b), 18, 123-131.

Carkhuff, R.R. *Cry Twice.* Amherst, Mass.: Human Resource Development Press, 1974 (a).

Carkhuff, R.R. *The Art of Problem-Solving.* Amherst, Mass.: Human Resource Development Press, 1974 (b).

Carkhuff, R.R. *The Art of Program Development.* Amherst, Mass.: Human Resource Development Press, 1975.

Carkhuff, R.R., and Alexik, M. The effects of the manipulation of client depth of self-exploration upon high and low functioning counselors. *Journal of Clinical Psychology,* 1967, 23, 210-212.

Carkhuff, R.R., and Anthony, W.A. *The Skills of Helping.* Amherst, Mass.: Human Resource Development Press, 1979.

Carkhuff, R.R., and Becker, J. *Toward Excellence in Education.* Amherst, Mass.: Carkhuff Institute of Human Technology, 1979.

Carkhuff, R.R., and Berenson, B.G. *Beyond Counseling and Therapy.* New York: Holt, Rinehart & Winston, 1967, 1977.

Carkhuff, R.R., and Berenson, B.G. *Teaching as Treatment.* Amherst, Mass.: Human Resource Development Press, 1976.

Carkhuff, R.R., and Bierman, R. Training as a preferred mode of treatment of parents of emotionally disturbed children. *Journal of Counseling Psychology.* 1970, 17, 157-161.

Carkhuff, R.R., and Pierce, R.M. *Helping Begins at Home,* Amherst, Mass.: Human Resource Development Press, 1976.

Collingwood, T. HRD model and physical fitness. In D.W. Kratochvil (Ed.), *HRD Model in Education.* Baton Rouge, La.: Southern Universtiy, 1972.

Collingwood, T., Douds, A., Williams, H., and Wilson, R. *Developing Youth Resources,* Amherst, Mass.: Carkhuff Institute of Human Technology, 1978.

Combs, A., Avila D., and Purkey, W. *Helping Relationships: Basic Concepts for the Helping Professions.* Boston: Allyn and Bacon, 1978.

Danish, S., and Hauer, A. *Helping Skills: A Basic Training Program.* New York: Behavioral Publications, 1973.

Egan, G. *The Skilled Helper.* Monterey, Cal.: Brooks, Cole, 1975.

Ekman, P., Friesen, W., and Ellworth, P. *Emotion in the Human Face.* New York: Pergammon, 1972.

Eysenck, H.J. The effects of psychotherapy. In H.J. Eysenck (Ed.), *The Handbook of Abnormal Psychology.* New York: Basic books, 1960.

Eysenck, H.J. The effects of psychotherapy. *International Journal of Psychotherapy,* 1965, 1, 99-178.

Freud, S. *New Introductory Lectures.* New York: Norton, 1933.

Fromm, E. *Man for Himself.* New York: Holt, Rinehart & Winston, 1947.

Garfield, S. Research on client variables in psychotherapy. In A.E. Bergin and S.L. Garfield (Eds.), *Handbook of Psychotherapy and Behavioral Change.* New York: Wiley & Sons, 1971.

Gazda, G. *Human Relations Development.* Boston: Allyn and Bacon, 1973.

Genther, R., and Moughan, J. Introverts' and extroverts' responses to non-verbal attending behavior. *Journal of Counseling Psychology,* 1977, 24, 144-146.

Genther, R., and Saccuzzo, D. Accuracy of perceptions of psychotherapeutic content as a function of observers' levels of facilitation. *Journal of Clinical Psychology,* 1977, 33, 517-519.

Ginzberg, E., Ginsburg, S.W., Axelrad, S., and Herma, J.L. *Occupational Choice.* New York: Columbia University Press, 1951.

Goldstein, A., Sprafkin, R., and Gershaw, N. *Skill Training for Community Living.* New York: Pergammon Press, 1976.

Gordon, R. *Interviewing: Strategy, Techniques and Tactics.* Homewood, Ill.: Dorsey Press, 1975.

Hackney, H., and Cornier, L. *Counseling Strategies and Objectives.* 2nd ed. Englewood Cliffs, N.J.: Prentice-Hall, 1979.

Hall, E. *The Silent Language.* New York: Doubleday, 1959.

Hall, E. *Beyond Culture.* New York: Doubleday, 1976.

Hefele, T.J. The effects of systematic human relations training upon student achievement. *Journal of Research and Development in Education,* 1971, 4, 52-69.

Heidegger, M. *Being and Time.* London: SCM Press, 1962.

Holder, T., Carkhuff, R.R., and Berenson, B.G. The differential effects of the manipulation of therapeutic conditions upon high and low functioning clients. *Journal of Counseling Psychology,* 1967, 14, 63-66.

Horney, K. *Our Inner Conflicts.* New York: Norton, 1945.

Ivey, A. The counselor as teacher. *Personnel and Guidance Journal,* 1976, 54, 431-434.

Ivey, A., and Authier, J. *Microcounseling.* Springfield, Ill.: Thomas, 1971, 1978.

Johnson, D. *Reaching Out: Interpersonal Effectiveness and Self-Actualization.* Englewood Cliffs, N.J.: Prentice-Hall, 1972.

Jung, C. *The Integration of the Personality.* New York: Holt, Rinehart & Winston, 1939.

Krasner, L., and Ullman, L. *Research in Behavior Modification.* New York: Holt, Rinehart & Winston, 1965.

Levitt, E.E. Psychotherapy with children: A further evaluation. *Behavior Research and Therapy,* 1963, 1, 45-51.

Lewis, W.W. Continuity and intervention in emotional disturbance: A review. *Exceptional Children,* 1965, 31, 465-475.

May, R. (Ed.). *Existential Psychology.* New York: Random House, 1961.

Mehrabian, A. *Nonverbal Communication.* New York: Aldine-Atherton, 1972.

Mickelson, D.J., and Stevic, R.R. Differential effects of facilitative and non-facilitative behavioral counselors. *Journal of Counseling Psychology,* 1971, 18, 314-319.

Montgomery, C., and Brown, A. *In the Land of the Blind.* Amherst, Mass.: Carkhuff Institute of Human Technology, 1980.

Okun, B. *Effective Helping: Interviewing and Counseling Techniques.* North Scituate, Mass.: Duxbury Press, 1976.

Pagell, W., Carkhuff, R.R., and Berenson, B.G. The predicted differential effects of the level of counselor functioning upon the level of functioning of out-patients. *Journal of Clinical Psychology,* 1967, 23, 510-512.

Parsons, F. *Choosing a Vocation.* Boston: Houghton Mifflin, 1909.

Patterson, C. *Theories of Counseling and Psychotherapy. 2nd ed.* New York: Harper & Row, 1973.

Piaget, G., Carkhuff, R.R., and Berenson, B.G. The development of skills in interpersonal functioning. *Counselor Education and Supervision,* 1968, 2, 102-106.

Pierce, R.M. and Drasgow, J. Teaching facilitative interpersonal functioning to psychiatric inpatients. *Journal of Counseling Psychology,* 1969, 16, 295-298.

Rank, O. *The Trauma of Birth.* New York: Harcourt, 1929.

Rogers, C., Gendlin, E., Keisler, D., and Truax, C. *The Therapeutic Relationship and Its Impact.* Westport, Conn.: Greenwood Press, 1967.

Schefflen, A. *Stream and Structure of Communication Behavior.* Bloomington, Ind.: Purdue University Press, 1969.

Smith-Hanen, S. Nonverbal behavior and counselor warmth and empathy. *Journal of Counseling Psychology,* 1977, 24, 84-91.

Sprinthall, N., and Mosher, R. Psychological education: A means to promote personal development during adolescence. *The Counseling Psychologist,* 1971, 2(4), 3-84.

Sullivan, H. The meaning of anxiety in psychiatry and life. *Psychiatry,* 1948, 11(1).

Super, D.E. *Appraising Vocational Fitness.* New York: Harper & Row, 1949.

Truax, C.B., and Carkhuff, R.R. *Toward Effective Counseling and Psychotherapy.* Chicago: Aldine, 1967.

Vitalo, R. The effects of facilitative interpersonal functioning in a conditioning paradigm. *Journal of Counseling Psychology,* 1970, 17, 141-144.

Watson, J.B. Behaviorism and the concept of mental disease. *Journal of Philosophical Psychology,* 1916, 13, 589-597.

Wolpe, J., Salter, A., and Renya, L. *The Conditioning Therapies.* New York: Holt, Rinehart & Winston, 1964.

APPENDIX C

ANNOTATED BIBLIOGRAPHY

Recent Research and Models

Carkhuff, R.R.
Sources of Human Productivity
Amherst, Mass.: Human Resource Development Press, 1983
> Useful for professionals in private as well as public sector agencies. Provides empirical base and models for relating human technology to human resource development and individual performance and, thus, organizational productivity. Describes policy-making, management, supervision and delivery functions and skills for human and educational service agencies as well as business and government.

Carkhuff, R.R.
Interpersonal Skills and Human Productivity
Amherst, Mass.: Human Resource Development Press, 1983.
> Useful for professionals in private as well as public sector agencies. Summarizes two decades of research of interpersonal skills in 164 studies of 158,884 recipients. Describes the effects of helper interpersonal skills as well as direct training of helpees upon outcome indices of helpee functioning in living, learning and working.

Carkhuff, R.R.
Toward Actualizing Human Potential
Amherst, Mass.: Human Resource Development Press, 1981
> Useful for professionals concerned with education and training. Provides models and skills for developing and organizing content and teaching methods and making the teaching delivery.

Research and Models

Anthony, W.A.
The Principles of Psychiatric Rehabilitation
Baltimore, Md.: University Park Press, 1979
Useful for professionals engaged in the practice of psychiatric rehabilitation in community mental health centers and clinics. Concludes that the key to successful psychiatric rehabilitation is the skill level of the practitioner, not where the helpee is treated. An outline of the skills necessary along with a summary of the research supporting each skill is also included.

Aspy, D.N. and Roebuck, F.N.
Kids Don't Learn from People They Don't Like
Amherst, Mass.: Human Resource Development Press, 1977
Useful for understanding the research base for the Carkhuff Model in teaching. Hundreds of teachers were trained in interpersonal skills. The effects on thousands of learners were studied. Significant gains were achieved on the following indices: student absenteeism and tardiness; student discipline and school crises; student learning skills and cognitive growth. Concludes that the Carkhuff Model is the preferred teacher training model.

Berenson, B.G.
Belly-to-Belly and Back-to-Back: The Militant Humanism of Robert R. Carkhuff
Amherst, Mass.: Human Resource Development Press, 1975
Useful for an understanding of the human assumptions underlying the human resource development models of Carkhuff. Presents a collection of prose and poetry by Carkhuff. Concludes by challenging us to die growing.

Berenson, B.G. and Carkhuff, R.R.
The Sources of Gain in Counseling and Psychotherapy
New York: Holt, Rinehart & Winston, 1967
Useful for an in-depth view of the different orientations to helping. Integrates the research of diverse approaches to helping. Concludes with a model of core conditions around which the different preferred modes of treatment make their own unique contributions to helpee benefits.

Berenson, B.G. and Mitchell, K.M.
Confrontation: For Better or Worse
Amherst, Mass.: Human Resource Development Press, 1974
Useful for an in-depth view of confrontation and immediacy as well as the core interpersonal dimensions. Presents extensive experimental manipulation of core interpersonal skills and confrontation and immediacy. Concludes that while confrontation is never necessary and never sufficient, in the hands of an effective helper, it may be efficient for moving the helpee toward constructive gain or change.

Carkhuff, R.R.
Helping and Human Relations. Vol. I Selection and Training. Vol II Practice and Research
New York: Holt, Rinehart & Winston, 1969
Useful for understanding the research base for interpersonal skills in counseling and education. Operationalizes the helping process in great detail. Presents extensive research evidence for systematic selection, training and treatment procedures. Concludes that teaching is the preferred mode of treatment for helping.

Carkhuff, R.R.
The Development of Human Resources
New York: Holt, Rinehart & Winston, 1971
Useful for understanding applications of human resource development (HRD) models. Describes and presents research evidence for numerous applications of helping skills training in human, educational and community resource development. Concludes that

systematic planning for human delivery systems can be
effectively translated into human benefits.

Carkhuff, R.R. and Becker, J.W.
Toward Excellence in Education
Amherst, Mass.: Carkhuff Institute of Human Technology,
1977
Useful for understanding the ingredients of effective
education, including: teachers; learners; parents; ad-
ministrators; and the community. Concludes that a
human technology is required to bridge the gap from
our concepts of teaching to our deliveries of learning.

Carkhuff, R.R. and Becker, J.W.
The Day the Schools Closed Down
Amherst, Mass.: Carkhuff Institute of Human Technology,
1978
Useful for understanding the interaction of different
systems affecting human resource development:
resource systems, government systems, economic
systems, and educational systems. Concludes that a
human achievement system based upon a human
technology can affect the other system constructively.

Carkhuff, R.R., Devine, J., Berenson, B.G., Griffin, A.H.,
Angelone, R., Keeling, T., Patch, W. and Steinberg, H.
Cry Twice!
Amherst, Mass.: Human Resource Development Press,
1974
Useful for understanding the ingredients of institutional
change. Details the people, programs and organizational variables needed to transform an institution from
a custodial to a treatment orientation. Concludes that institutional change begins with people change.

Collingwood, T., Douds, A., Williams, H., and Wilson, R.D.
Developing Youth Resources Through Police Diversion
Amherst, Mass.: Carkhuff Institute of Human Technology,
1978
Useful for understanding the effective ingredients of
delinquency prevention and youth rehabilitation. The
purpose of the program described was to provide

services at the police level to juvenile offenders in order to reduce recidivism by delivering skills training and by monitoring services to youth and parents. Concludes that with systematic skills training programs, with skilled personnel, and with an organizational framework in a police department, you can make a dramatic and constructive impact on juvenile offender recidivism.

Carkhuff, R.R. and Berenson, B.G.
Beyond Counseling and Therapy
New York: Holt, Rinehart & Winston, Second Edition, 1977
Useful for understanding of the core interpersonal conditions and their implications and applications. Adds many core dimensions and factors them out as responsive and initiative dimensions. Includes an analysis of the client-centered, existential, psychoanalytic, trait-and-factor and behavioristic orientations to counseling and psychotherapy. Concludes that only the trait-and-factor and behavioristic positions make unique contributions to human benefits over and above the core conditions.

Carkhuff, R.R. and Berenson, B.G.
Teaching as Treatment
Amherst, Mass.: Human Resource Development Press, 1976
Useful for understanding the development of a human technology. Operationalizes the helping process as teaching. Offers research evidence for living, learning and working skills development and physical, emotional and intellectual outcomes. Concludes that learning-to-learn is the fundamental model for living, learning and working.

Rogers, C.R., Gendlin, E.T., Kiesler, D. and Truax, C.B.
The Therapeutic Relationship and Its Impact
Madison, Wis.: University of Wisconsin Press, 1967
Useful for understanding the historical roots of the HRD models. Presents extensive evidence on client-centered counseling for schizophrenic patients. Concludes that core interpersonal dimensions of empathy, regard and congruence are critical to effective helping.

Truax, C.B. and Carkhuff, R.R.
Toward Effective Counseling and Therapy
Chicago: Aldine, 1967
> Useful for understanding the transitional phases in developing HRD models. Presents extensive evidence on training lay and professional helpers as well as different orientations to helping. Concludes that the core interpersonal dimensions of empathy, respect and genuineness are critical to effective helping.

Skills Development and Applications

LIVING SKILLS

Carkhuff, R.R.
The Art of Helping V—Trainer's Guide
Amherst, Mass.: Human Resource Development Press, 1983
> Useful training techniques for teaching helpers. Includes attending, responding, personalizing and initiating learning exercises with counseling applications.

Carkhuff, R.R., et al.
The Art of Helping V—Student Workbook
Amherst, Mass.: Human Resource Development Press, 1983
> Useful for bridging the gap between reading about helping skills in the text and practicing the skills in training sessions. Includes more than one hundred practice exercises for attending, responding, personalizing and initiating skills.

Carkhuff, R.R. and Anthony, W.A.
The Skills of Helping
Amherst, Mass.: Human Resource Development Press, 1979
> Useful for training helpers in helping skills. Includes attending, responding, personalizing, problem-solving, program development and initiating skills.

Carkhuff, R.R.
The Art of Problem-Solving
Amherst, Mass.: Human Resource Development Press, 1973

Useful for developing decision-making skills. Includes modules on defining problems and goals and selecting and implementing courses of action.

Carkhuff, R.R.
The Art of Program Development
Amherst, Mass.: Human Resource Development Press, 1974
Useful for developing program development skills. Includes modules on defining goals and developing and implementing programs to achieve the goals.

TEACHING SKILLS

Carkhuff, R.R., Berenson, D.H. and Pierce, R.M.
The Skills of Teaching: Interpersonal Skills
Amherst, Mass.: Human Resource Development Press, 1977
Useful for preservice and inservice teachers. Includes attending, responding, personalizing and initiating modules with classroom applications.

Berenson, D.H., Carkhuff, R.R. and Pierce, R.M.
The Skills of Teaching—Teacher's Guide
Amherst, Mass.: Human Resource Development Press, 1977
Useful training skills for teacher trainers. Includes methods for developing content and delivering interpersonal skills modules.

Berenson, D.H., Berenson, S.R., and Carkhuff, R.R.
The Skills of Teaching: Content Development Skills
Amherst, Mass.: Human Resource Development Press, 1978
Useful for both preservice and inservice teacher education. Includes how to develop and organize both yearly and daily teaching content and how to identify skills and the steps needed to do them, along with the facts, concepts and principles students will need to perform these skills.

Berenson, D.H., Berenson, S.R., and Carkhuff, R.R.
The Skills of Teaching: Lesson Planning Skills
Amherst, Mass.: Human Resource Development Press,
1978
> Useful for teaching both preservice and inservice
> teachers. Includes how to select a piece of content and
> develop a lesson plan to deliver it using teaching
> methods to review, overview, present, practice and
> summarize.

Berenson, S.R., Berenson, D.H. and Carkhuff, R.R.
The Skills of Teaching: Teaching Delivery Skills
Amherst, Mass.: Human Resource Development Press,
1979
> Useful for both inservice and preservice teacher educa-
> tion programs. Includes a summary and integrative
> presentation of content development skills, lesson plan-
> ning skills and interpersonal skills as applied to actual
> teaching delivery.

WORKING SKILLS

Carkhuff, R.R. and Friel, T.W.
The Art of Developing a Career—Student's Guide
Amherst, Mass.: Human Resource Development Press,
1974
> Useful for developing careers. Includes modules on ex-
> panding, narrowing and planning for career alternatives.

Carkhuff, R.R., Pierce, R.M., Friel, T.W. and Willis, D.
GETAJOB
Amherst, Mass.: Human Resource Development Press,
1975
> Useful for developing placement skills. Includes
> modules on finding jobs, preparing resumes and han-
> dling job interviews.

Friel, T.W. and Carkhuff, R.R.
The Art of Developing a Career—Helper's Guide
Amherst, Mass.: Human Resource Development Press,
1974
> Useful training skills for helpers and teachers.

Includes methods for involving the learners in exploring, understanding and acting upon their careers.

FITNESS SKILLS

Collingwood, T. and Carkhuff, R.R.
Get Fit for Living
Amherst, Mass.: Human Resource Development Press, 1976
Useful for developing physical fitness. Includes modules for self-assessing, setting goals and developing and implementing fitness programs.

Collingwood, T. and Carkhuff, R.R.
Get Fit for Living—Trainer's Guide
Amherst, Mass.: Human Resource Development Press, 1976
Useful training skills for fitness trainers. Includes methods and programs for delivering fitness skills.

APPLICATIONS

Anthony, W.A. and Carkhuff, R.R.
The Art of Health Care
Amherst, Mass.: Human Resource Development Press, 1976
Useful for health care workers. Includes modules and applications of interpersonal, decision-making and program development skills in health care facilities.

Anthony, W.A., Cohen, M.R., Pierce, R.M., Cannon, J.R., Cohen, B.F., Friel, T.W., Spaniol, L. and Vitalo, R.L.
The Psychiatric Rehabilitation Practice Series (6 vols. and instructor's guide) Baltimore, Md.: University Park Press, 1979
Useful for inservice and preservice training of psychiatric rehabilitation practitioners. Includes volumes on diagnostic planning, rehabilitation programming, professional evaluation, career counseling, career placement and community service coordination.

Carkhuff, R.R. and Pierce, R.M.
Teacher as Person
Washington, D.C.: National Education Association, 1976
Useful for teachers interested in multi-cultural education. Includes modules and applications of interpersonal skills in the school.

Carkhuff, R.R. and Pierce, R.M.
Helping Begins at Home
Amherst, Mass.: Human Resource Development Press, 1976
Useful for parents interested in parenting skills. Includes modules and applications of interpersonal and program development skills in the home.

The books in the preceding Annotated Bibliography can be purchased directly from the publishers:

Aldine Publishing Company
529 South Wabash Ave.
Chicago, IL 60605

Carkhuff Institute of Human Technology
22 Amherst Road
Amherst, MA 01002

Holt, Rinehart & Winston
383 Madison Ave.
New York, NY 10019

Human Resource Development Press
22 Amherst Rd.
Amherst, MA 01002

National Education Association
Distribution Center
West Haven, CT 06516

University Park Press
233 E. Redwood St.
Baltimore, MD 21202

INDEX